Step Up

Step Up

STEP-PARENTING AND THE ART OF CREATING A HEALTHY, HAPPY, BLENDED FAMILY

Katherine Walker

Author's note: all case studies in the book are anonymised composite cases, to protect the privacy of my clients and contributors.

First published in 2025 by Headline Home, an imprint of Headline Publishing Group

2

Cataloguing in Publication Data is available from the British Library

Trade paperback ISBN 978 10 35412 11 2
eISBN 978 10 35412 13 6

Typeset in Dante by CC Book Production

Printed and bound in Great Britain by Clays Ltd, Elcograf S.p.A.

Headline's policy is to use papers that are natural, renewable and recyclable products and made from wood grown in well-managed forests and other controlled sources. The logging and manufacturing processes are expected to conform to the environmental regulations of the country of origin.

Headline Publishing Group Limited
An Hachette UK Company
Carmelite House
50 Victoria Embankment
London EC4Y 0DZ

The authorized representative in the EEA is Hachette Ireland,
8 Castlecourt Centre, Dublin 15, D15 XTP3, Ireland
(email: info@hbgi.ie)

www.headline.co.uk
www.hachette.co.uk

Pierre Teilhard de Chardin said 'we are not human beings seeking a spiritual experience, we are spiritual beings having a human experience'. So to all those currently rocking the very human experience of being part of a step or blended family . . . a high five. And to all those who may be struggling, a helping hand instead.

Contents

Introduction

Forming a blended or step-family can be incredibly exciting and rewarding. However, the process is loaded with emotional and practical complexity, especially when compared to the arguably simpler 'nuclear' construct, where all the children are born to the same two parents. In nuclear families, there are fewer people involved, the family type is far more traditional (historically speaking), and so generally viewed by society as 'the norm'. Plus, much of the time, this variety of family isn't characterised by divided loyalties and bruised egos – in the beginning, at least.

So, unless your new blended family is built on strong foundations, dysfunctional relationships within it can potentially wreak havoc on our self-esteem, sense of belonging and identity. When it feels 'right', however, the emerging family unit has the potential to enable learning, growth, teaching and healing. It has the capacity to be a source of both joy and inspiration, and be something that you can take pride in having created and being a part of.

Who is this book for?

Many resources on this subject focus on, or are written for, the step-parent – often specifically the step-mother. And yet the step-parent is just one member of a very complex family type, and to focus only on them implies that they should both be responsible for making things work and also scapegoated at the first sign of trouble. This, reader, is not fair.

So, this book is for *anyone* who is part of either a step-family, where the new couple haven't had children together, but where at least one of the couple has had them in a previous relationship, or a blended family, where the new couple have also had at least one child together. As the definitions are nuanced (and not widely understood), for ease throughout the book I have predominantly used the term 'blended family' to describe both step and blended combinations. This includes people who weren't necessarily looking to start or join a blended family, but who perhaps, during their adulthood, have found themselves falling in love with someone who has kids. Or maybe you are separated/divorced with children of your own, and, necessarily, whoever you go on to meet will be a part of their lives. People in these situations often begin with good intentions but later find themselves floundering, or perhaps even worse – trying to re-create a nuclear family construct only to be left frustrated and confused.

Step Up is also for people who have always been a part of a blended family, but perhaps one where the blended family potential has never been maximised, because one or all of its members haven't thought consciously about its formation, how it would evolve, how to maintain it, or how to deal appropriately with rupture and repair. Or maybe you had a difficult experience growing up in a blended family, and now, in your adulthood, you're looking for an opportunity to reset and to minimise the potentially negative impact of your earlier experience on your current situation.

Step Up is also suitable for young adults who are perhaps part of a blended family, by virtue of having one or more step-parents. If that's you, maybe you've struggled with being a part of this complex arrangement, and would like to understand a little more about what's happening from a psychological point of view, just beneath the surface.

Why now?

Having read the literature that's readily accessible today, I find it incredible that such an important aspect of our society doesn't have more resources available to offer support to those navigating it. And it is all the more eyebrow raising when we consider that, by 2021, there were already well over three quarters of a million step and blended families in the UK alone, according to the Office for National Statistics. This number may well be under-represented, given the complexities of gathering and interpreting the relevant information. However, as the numbers of blended families are likely to only increase overtime, there has never been a better time to expand the range of resources available.

Let's take a closer look, so we're all on the same page here. UK data is gathered through the census, which happens once a decade – and we all know how much can change in this time. The data people choose to share in those surveys relies on self-disclosure, which means it's based on how respondents choose to self-identify, and categorise their family. For a whole host of reasons, people may not identify as being part of a step or blended family. A lack of willing, or understanding of the subtle differences between categories and definitions, are just the tip of the iceberg. Take the illustrative case of the self-identified single mother with a long-term partner, for example. This couple haven't begun to co-habit yet, and aren't thinking of marriage. Technically, she would be considered part of a lone or single parent family – yet she and her children may be interacting with her partner on a daily basis, and said partner may have a significant influence on their lives. And so on.

While the numbers of families like this aren't insignificant, they by no means make up the majority, so they tend to be under-represented in the media, and in the film and entertainment industries. Plus they're often kept in the shadows – sometimes even incorrectly, and sadly, perceived by some as a shady result of 'failed marriages', which can be demoralising and stigmatising. Firstly, failure may not be how you see things at all, so this is quite the value judgement to take on board. Secondly, to talk about the blended family as a result of the previous relationship failing almost implies that the blended family only exists because the previous, societially 'acceptable', relationship has broken down. Implicit in this is the notion, therefore, that the new adult relationship is somehow secondary – and so the 'othering' begins! All this is reinforced very subtly – blink-and-you-miss-it-type stuff – but this nuanced implication is an important one which affects our blended families, and perhaps contributes to people, at times, shying away from identifying as being part of their own. Consequently, as a minority group, there are fewer resources to support such families, and so the cycle continues.

However, when the adults in the mix take the time to *consciously* create the right conditions – by which I mean a safe and loving environment, with a good helping of fun on the side – growth can follow for all. Not just for the children, who may still be young and highly impressionable, but for the adults too. Far from being some-thing to keep in the shadows, I believe that a blended family brings its own unique opportunity to create something new that may even be *consciously* sought after, and created based on solid life experience rather than arguably naive ideals; combining the collective wisdom and values of everyone within it. But maybe you're already aware of these positives, given you're taking the time to read this?

Why me?

The topic of blended families has fascinated me for over thirty years. I have been a member of no less than three of them, from my childhood onwards, in a number of roles – from being step-daughter to both a step-mother and a step-father, to becoming a step-mother in adulthood. Just like you, I have personally experienced the highs and the lows blended families can bring.

In my professional life too, as a practising psychotherapist, coach and mediator, I am privileged to work with a wide variety of individuals, couples, and groups, on a diverse range of topics to do with mental health, conflict resolution, relational dynamics and performance optimisation. Yet, as a result of my personal understanding and experience, it is blended families that I return to again and again. It's a special area of interest that continues to capture my heart and mind, which led to it becoming not only the subject of my MA, and the main topic of my blog, but also the focus for what you are about to read.

Why not write a book for children, surely they're the ones who suffer?

I'm often asked why I don't work with children more broadly in my role as a psychotherapist. The reason for this is the same reason this book is primarily written for adults. I find that both children *and* adults tend to suffer when adults – the ones with mature brains (though not necessarily with more maturity!) and more power in the world – don't take responsibility for past hurts. They consequently take out their negative feelings in a destructive way on those around them, and so aren't able to equip little ones with the right tools to deal with what's to come. In a blended family this is particularly apparent. So I choose to work with the adults, and, in helping them become more self-aware and take responsibility, my hope is that the children in their care will benefit too.

Stepping into a blended world

There are many types of blended family. I aim for *Step Up* to be as inclusive as possible, and so we'll have a look at a wide variety of examples and situations. However, I want to be clear that, given our own uniqueness, and the differences found in every family, this book simply can't be a reflection of everyone's experience.

A flavour of blended family complexity

When compared to a nuclear family construct, the blended family has added complexities to contend with, which can be both practical and emotional in nature. These feelings and complicated dynamics may be actively or indirectly expressed by any number of people – both within and outside of the family. Let's name a few to build a picture of what we're up against:

- The thoughts the parent(s) have about the concept of separation and divorce, and their feelings about the specific circumstances of their own personal experience of divorce/separation.
- The parent's experience of their previous relationship, the areas

in which they might like to 'do things differently' second time around, and the elements they may want to stay (broadly!) the same.

- The feelings the ex-partner has about the fact their partner is moving on with another person, and to what extent they choose to express all or some of these in front of the children.
- The age of the children, whether they are still dependent on their parents, and the co-parenting, living and custody arrangements.
- The attitudes of the grandparents to the idea of divorce/separation in general, to the idea their son/daughter has separated from their wife or husband, their views on the new partner and to what extent they choose to express all or some of these in front of the children.
- The views and attitudes of the children's school friends, or the couple's social circle.
- The broader cultural backdrop of the blended family – community norms, the role (if any) that religion has to play.
- To what extent the new couple come from a similar background to one another, hold similar values, and how the respective values of the adults in the equation affect the children.
- If both adults are bringing children to the family, to what extent do their respective parenting values and behaviours align.
- The wider historical stereotypical views of blended families, and specifically the notoriety of one particular member of it – the step-mother. Oh, she gets a bad rap, doesn't she? More on her later. But . . . spoiler alert: we all need to give her a break.

. . . And so on. I'm sure you could think of plenty more without too much trouble. These dynamics are always running in the background, but to what extent they affect the family will depend on each individual group. Simply being aware of these additional complexities when you're creating your own blended family will do much to help everyone consciously adjust to what you and your partner want your 'new normal' to be. And by reading this book you will learn to acknowledge the bravery and strength it takes to be part of a blended family.

I have written *Step Up* from a few different perspectives. Firstly, relationships. The groundwork is laid by looking at what might be going on for the individuals (both the grownups and kids) that define the family. Then, we will go on to look at the group as a whole, and finally we'll take a look at some of the nuances of the inter-family relationships.

Secondly, we go on a bit of a practical journey through the blended family life cycle. From exploring life in the early stages – when to make introductions and how best to handle them, how to bring the family together, and how to handle various milestones – we then move on to the establishment of norms, roles and rituals, as well as how to deal with things when they go wrong in more established blended families. Towards the end, we'll take a closer look at what happens when a blended family breaks down – the benefits of reparations and how to handle separations.

Helpful tips vs finding your own way

This subject brings up so much for so many – blended families are a hugely emotive topic. It's hard to make rational decisions when we're feeling particularly emotional, so it's unsurprising that people often tell me they sometimes struggle to know what to do for the best in their own blended families. Because of this, I have deliberately written *Step Up* to include plenty of examples in order to illustrate the points being made, and also some tips and experiences from people in real blended families.

The examples and anecdotes shared throughout are necessarily based on a relatively small number of people's direct experiences – but each theme, without exception, has been echoed to me again and again by others over time. I work at depth with my clients, and my job means I deal in the language of sentiment and subjectivity. These experiences are valuable, and, in fact, through storytelling we make meaning, learning from and about each other in order to raise our collective understanding and awareness. But I would welcome plenty of further research of all kinds in this area; it is only by shining a light on such a complex topic that we will help to make blended families as successful, healthy and commonly accepted as possible.

A little bit about inclusivity

I'm writing this book from the perspective of being a white, cis gender female living in the UK, with decades of personal and professional experience of helping blended families and being part of them myself. The language of this book will be of its time, and in a few years will no doubt become dated. I am aware of the complex issues related to race, social class, and gender that will affect your own identity, as well as that of your unique blended family, to some degree. We know that not everyone identifies with the sex they were assigned at birth, and furthermore we naturally all have our own unique views on the concept of gender, as well as the differences we perceive between the binary concepts of the masculine and the feminine.

First and foremost, however, this book is an exploration of blended families, and in writing it I have found I cannot do the subject matter justice, or make the book easily comprehensible, without referring to the more traditional understanding we have of gender roles and norms and by using gender normative terms. On that note, I am also conscious that most of the case studies used depict heterosexual partnerships, which is reflective of the majority of blended families I come across.

If what you're about to read gives you 'all the answers', then great! This is unlikely to be the case, however, as your circumstances are unique to you. I am nevertheless confident that *Step Up* will at least give you and your partner plenty of food for thought and an opportunity for self-reflection. You will both learn to take the time to think carefully about what is right for you, your relationship, your children and step-children. My invitation to you is to take what you need from it. Maybe you'll put into practice some of the suggestions I make, or simply take on board only the principles we talk through, instead finding your own solutions. Either is fine. Most importantly, you will realise that while making mistakes is inevitable, it's okay to do so and you need to cut yourself some slack sometimes – life is for learning. Your best is always good enough and there is no such thing as perfect.

1

Understanding the Grownups

The one who got divorced

This isn't a book about divorce or separation. However, as these sensitive events are, for one of you at least, the precursors to the creation of our blended families, we simply can't ignore the impact they have. So, reader, let's get started by saying a few words on this topic.

When people settle down with the person of their dreams, they rarely expect that one day it will end. The prospect of future separation doesn't motivate commitment, particularly one that is legal and binding – when to peel apart the lives you have created together will cost time, money, and emotional labour. And yet . . . We all know the stats. These days 41% of marriages end in divorce before their twenty-fifth anniversary. Shocking. Or . . . is it?

The quality of our long-term relationships arguably have the power to affect us more than any other. Marriages are made for all sorts of reasons – so, for clarity, I'm not talking here about arranged marriages or those of convenience. I'm talking about love matches, where we choose our partner. Time progresses, and what we want and need changes as we get older and (hopefully!) wiser. Consequently, unless we're deeply in sync with our partner, we can begin to outgrow one another. When a marriage or long-term relationship breaks down, regardless of whether there are children involved, it is usually desperately sad.

It's sad, but it's also okay – providing you treat yourself and your soon to be ex-spouse or ex-partner with respect in the process. Far better to recognise now, than continue to live a life that makes you miserable, or prevents you from growing. Giving yourself permission to make a change, and the chance to realise your hopes and dreams, either living a single life or one with a new partner, is one of the greatest gifts you can give yourself.

The prospect of making such a move can be incomprehensible for many. We fear the unknown, letting people down, reputational damage, being worse off financially and so on. These things, and much more, hold people back from giving themselves permission to make the changes necessary to support their happiness, goals, and the life they want for themselves. Consequently, for many, separation can for years be nothing more than a distant, unattainable pipedream.

So what happens to those who do have the courage to call time on their relationship? Well, it can take a long time to recover. And when those relationships produce children, it naturally brings a raft of extra considerations that generate a far greater emotional burden compared to those that don't. How will the kids respond initially, and consequently adjust? What kind of lifestyle will they now be able to have? Will any differences in parenting styles mean the children receive mixed messages from you both, once you reside in separate homes?

Telling the children

Acknowledging it's better to make a change is only the first step. Once you have made the difficult decision to separate from your partner and co-parent, you will undoubtedly think about how to share the news with the children. Don't rush this; however fraught your relationship is, spending some time to align on the narrative you plan to share will be helpful for both them and you, when you come to have the conversation. Starting with some of the practical considerations will help – put yourself in the kids' shoes. They'll want to know where they'll be living. The reason for your break up. How quickly will Mum/Dad be moving out. Will the house be sold?

Alignment is important, as it will set the tone for how significant parts of this process will be handled by you both, as the family unit starts to separate. Creating as much stability as possible, in a time typically characterised by instability, will pay dividends for the psychological health of the children in the future.

For the conversation itself, as Natasha shares below, it's important you apply the same principles for each child. Telling the kids together, and at the same time, will mean they hear the same messages, and show them that you are aligned (which I get you might not feel deep down). It's important the children don't take on unnecessary feelings of needing to protect the parent they perceive to be reluctant to separate, or start feeling angry with the parent they perceive to be instigating the split. These feelings are for you and your ex to deal with, as adults. Emotional and practical support, if you need it, can be sought from friends, family, or a trusted therapist/other professional – not the children.

My parents separated when I was really young, and both went on to remarry. I vividly remember Mum telling my older brothers one weekend when I was with Dad, and his job was to tell me. It was strange, and I've never understood why – maybe we even got different versions of it? So, right from the start it set the tone – I felt a bit separated from my siblings as far as our parent's separation was concerned. Like we were on different journeys with it – and I was by myself. I wish they had told us all together.

Natasha, stepdaughter, daughter and mother (34)

You can see here how your identity as a parent will be impacted by the separation process. But your personal identity will also be affected. All of these considerations and many more besides will bring about a complex set of feelings in you, as the parent ready to move on, for example, and perhaps begin afresh with someone new. Feelings can include:

Relief
Shame
Pride
Excitement
Peace
Anxiety
Worry
Fear
And perhaps most commonly and unhelpfully of all –
the Big G: Guilt.

Guilt is defined in two main ways – as a noun we refer to a *state* of guilt that results from having committed a recognised crime of some kind, legal or otherwise. But in this case, used as a verb, it describes a negative feeling induced in someone for a *perceived* or *implied* sense of wrongdoing. We are, of course, quite capable of feeling guilty all by ourselves, but often guilty feelings can be induced in an individual as a result of another's inability to take responsibility for their own difficult feelings. Consequently, they hold that person responsible for the negativity they carry. In the case of divorce, we often hear accusations bandied about, such as: *'You're to blame here, you're the one who wants to leave – not me!'* . . . *'You're the one who took that job and who is away all the time, everything was great until then – you can take full responsibility for the marriage ending.'* I call it being given someone's 'emotional suitcases' to carry.

When marriages or long-term relationships end, early conversations are often limited to fault or blame, which is exhausting and reductive – it doesn't change the fact the relationship is ending. More worryingly, fault and blame prevent both sides from acknowledging and taking responsibility for whatever might have been going on that is theirs to own. Whether, in this particular instance, that meant one or both parties weren't getting what they needed, weren't happy or satisfied, or lacked the skills or desire to bring these concerns back into the relationship to talk them through properly. Usually one side takes on too little responsibility, while the other takes on far too much.

The all too frequent tendency is to buy into the toxic cocktail of fear, guilt and blame, which clouds a parent's ability to form their new blended family alongside their new partner of choice, consciously and healthily. Difficult feelings are avoided, new partners can be scapegoated, and people jump into unsuitable relationships to prove a point or seek revenge, resulting in boundaries not being established effectively.

Custody and living arrangements

Difficult decisions regarding child-care agreements will also need to be made during this initial period, and although, of course, everyone wants new living arrangements to stabilise quickly, in some ways this is a shame, as emotions often run too high to make the most balanced of decisions. As a result, arrangements may end up being informed – partly, at least – by guilty feelings, and not wanting to be judged for deviating from cultural norms.

Often one party can end up taking on too much responsibility, which can cause unhelpful longer-term ripples within our blended families. But it works both ways. The parent who spends the least proportion of time with the kids post-separation is often the father (in today's world at least). Less time can equal a feeling of less power, which is also problematic. Consequently, the father can often have concerns that he will lose what custody he does have, and/or that the children will be turned against him. To avoid this a propensity to display compensating and colluding behaviours can develop – tolerating the children's negative behaviours, say, or pacifying his ex-partner to avoid his fears coming true. Yet such fear doesn't serve a useful purpose overall – both compensating and colluding are highly detrimental to the blended family.

Needless to say, there are lots of very good reasons why majority custody will often fall to one parent over another, so this is not an invitation for the pendulum to swing a different way just for the sake of it. Instead, right from the start, I simply encourage separating couples to consciously consider what's truly right for them, and for the children, without overly concerning themselves with fitting in with what's traditionally been the status quo.

This subject is, of course, a sensitive one – and I certainly don't want to give the impression that mums everywhere are fighting tooth and nail to keep fathers from their children. Indeed, I speak to many mums who would frankly love for there to be a lot more balance, but where dad cites an inflexible job/need to retain breadwinner status/ busy life/a flat that's too small for this to be the case, all of which can be frustrating.

Regardless of the specific dynamic of each former nuclear family, we cannot deny that, much of the time, majority custody falls with mum – and it cannot be the case that every separated couple everywhere is satisfied with this arrangement. So it stands to reason that a little more conscious conversation about the *real* reasons behind the decisions that are made at this crucial juncture may mean we don't typically default to stereotypical expectations of mum ending up with majority custody. This leaves dad to fulfil career/breadwinner aspirations and his ex-partner to fulfil a maternal archetypal role, both of which they and 'society' have arguably been conditioned to expect and accept without challenge, regardless of personal and private views. Whisper it, but isn't that a bit . . . old fashioned?

If you need to move forward but are struggling to reach consensus together, based on the fact your relationship has irrevocably broken down, then consider an intervention like mediation to help you come up with the custody arrangements that are right for you. Your mediator, especially if they are psychologically informed, will be skilled at working with you both separately, at an emotionally sensitive time, to help you both hear one another and to reach a resolution that works for all your needs.

It may be that, through your own conscious conversations, you and your co-parent decide to do things in stages before you settle on your preferred scenario, to help the children adjust or to accommodate practical realities, such as house/flat purchases and moves. This is a great way to put the children first and to ensure you, as the adults, also get your needs met. If you transition to your 'new normal' in stages, do give the kids as much awareness as possible about how things are going to play out. This way, everyone goes into it with eyes wide open about upcoming changes.

In the early stages, some separating couples choose to adopt a birdnesting strategy, where the children continue to live in the family home, and their (separating) parents take it in turns to move in and look after them. On paper this can seem like the ideal scenario, saving money and limiting emotional fallout. In reality, however, this can be *very* emotionally taxing for the parents, who are understandably keen to minimise uneccessary upheaval or instability for the sake of their children. Yet, they can find this temporary dynamic actually ends up exacerbating what is often already a strained relationship at this point. For example, having to negotiate new boundaries to alternately occupy the living spaces as harmoniously as possible, in a home they both used to share as a couple – not to mention trying to deal with the psychological impact of the relationship ending on top of all that – can create extra stress. It's not hard to imagine that moving out of the family home afresh, every other week, could even be a retraumatising experience for each member of the couple, providing a regular symbolic reminder of the original separation.

Depending on how long the arrangement continues, the process of then trying to meet someone, and begin a new relationship, can also present tricky challenges for the separating couple. What's more, even if a new partner is happy to accept these arrangements, there will likely be a degree of needing to keep this aspect of life compartmentalised until the former couple have moved to the next stage of their separation.

It can be confusing for the children too, as the nuclear family structure is still being preserved in many respects – especially if one parent used to be away overnight regularly anyway. As such, you may find that their ability to express and process their feelings about the separation are delayed somewhat, until they themselves are spending time in each of their (parents') new homes. So, while birdnesting can seem like an incredibly practical and convenient solution in the short term, just keep in mind that this approach doesn't change the fact the relationship has ended; ultimately it may take longer for all of you to settle and stabilise in the long run than it otherwise would have done.

However you decide to organise things, though, you can't ever think too hard about the practical reality of your set up, given it will directly affect the wellbeing of everyone involved, in particular that of the kids who can't decide for themselves. For example, if one parent ends up with majority custody, they are likely to be bound by geographical proximity to schools, which the other parent won't be restricted by. This can lead to one parent moving much farther away, meaning the kids will be forced to travel long distances to maintain contact – what I call 'shuttling'. Shuttling can be upsetting for the kids, as it reinforces the sense of separateness, and the frustration can put them off wanting to make the trip, particularly when they're a bit older, with their own social lives. If you are able to, consider living relatively close by to your co-parent to make travelling in between less arduous.

The same goes for kids having to pack entire suitcases for each weekend visit, or during school holidays. This can be upsetting, time-consuming, not to mention inconvenient when they're a bit older. So where possible and where finances permit, consider dupli-cating key items, and creating a dedicated private space, such as a bedroom, in both parents' homes. The alternative is having one main home and even one main parent – and therefore one occasional parent and one occasional place to visit. Unless handled very carefully, this can generate an avoidable sense of not belonging and not being wanted, as well as an avoidable parental hierarchy.

When I was separating from my ex-wife, the expectation was (reinforced by both her family and social circle) that we would end with an arrangement where I only saw my kids every other weekend. But I never wanted to be a weekend dad. I wanted equal custody, shared with my ex. She is a great mum and has a great relationship with them. But I too love my kids and I wanted to provide for them both emotionally and financially – and, most importantly, it's clear they need me too. We had so many hard conversations about it. We did it gradually, for the sake of the whole dynamic, but in the end we moved to a 50/50 balance, and haven't looked back. I feel we are a united co-parent team, both putting the kids first and looking after our own interests following our divorce. I really look forward to my weeks with the kids, and we have never been closer.

Chris, father (48)

In summary, a more balanced approach to living arrangements can benefit everyone's mental health:

- Dad gets an opportunity to deepen and maintain all-important bonds with his children throughout their childhood and adolescence.
- Mum gets a much needed break and an opportunity to regain her adult identity, which is broader than her role as parent.
- The kids have a greater sense of balance and harmony, which is hugely beneficial to the development of their young psyches.

Managing your own difficult feelings

As you navigate this process, I would encourage you to adopt the mindset of *empathising* with and *acknowledging* your own sadness and grief, as well as that of your former partner, as you go through the separation. You might be grieving too, over the fact the family structure you were previously a part of is changing, and your feelings about this may be completely different to those you may experience about the relationship ending. But also acknowledge that, while relationship breakdowns are generally awful for all those involved, you are far from alone. We are programmed both to seek safety and to grow, and where these conditions aren't met in one relationship, we're meant to go on to seek another we hope can give us what we've been missing. Endings and beginnings are a normal part of life – just as with birth there is death.

Acceptance of this cycle is in itself incredibly liberating. You begin to understand that by virtue of you or your former partner having had the courage to call time, you have now both been gifted a huge opportunity: to firstly find a place of internal safety, before going on to meet someone who affords you the space and respect to grow into the best version of yourself possible, someone with whom you can build a new family, together with your respective children.

Don't be afraid to make a change. Lots of people couldn't understand when I separated from the father of my toddler, many years ago. But I thought: why allow my children to grow up in an unhappy home, where we were arguing regularly? Staying would have actually caused more upset in the long run, and wouldn't have been good for the kids. I could easily have felt incredibly guilty, but it wouldn't have been helpful.

We just weren't compatible. If you have kids, it's ultimately better for them to have two happy parents moving on, both healing then finding new relationships, than being together and miserable. By valuing yourself, and separating from an unhappy relationship, you will teach your children to value themselves also.

Suzie, mother in a blended family (40)

Step-parents

If you're already a step-parent, how did you feel when you first found out your partner had children? Perhaps you already have kids yourself, and, if so, you may now be wondering when might be the right time to introduce them to your partner's kids. Or are you keen to have children yourself at some point, but for whatever reason it hasn't been the right time? You mightn't have intended to have kids at all, but didn't bank on falling for someone who already had them. However you feel will also be impacted by your partner's views. Do they want more children? How do they feel about the fact you do/do not have children? What are their views on how quickly they want to progress the relationship, given they have children?

No two blended families are the same. For the 'first time around-ers', with no responsibilities or dependents other than, say, the cat they once rescued together, the business of falling in (and out of) love is arguably a relatively uncomplicated proposition. For you, on the other hand, meeting someone with children, the prospect of deepening that connection and bringing the family together may be daunting, exciting, burdensome, overwhelming, or maybe even a source of joy.

It's likely to be a bit of a 'feeling soup', with everything in the mix all at once.

So it's no wonder that friends may warn you how hard it will be – or even share with you a spectacularly irritating and unhelpful opinion, such as *'I don't how you do it – I couldn't be with a person who has children – far too complicated for me!'* These comments are generally delivered in a slightly awestruck tone, and yet it's not hard to feel ever so slightly like you're going mad to even *consider* the prospect of settling down with a person who has children. What may have been intended as a compliment can feel a little backhanded!

The 'good enough' step-parent

It's important to take the views of others with a pinch of salt, and not let them derail your positive feelings about the relationship. It is undeniably true that to be a part of a successfully adjusted blended family takes a gargantuan amount of effort. But given we rely on our relationships to survive, what makes us think we lack the will necessary to learn to be a 'good enough' step-parent? I say 'good enough' deliberately – striving to be perfect turns the process into a competition, and opens the door for self-judgement. Neither of those things are the aims of our game, and they are also wholly unrealistic given the challenges blended families inevitably face as they form.

Being 'good enough' is a phrase I've borrowed from Donald Winnicott, a paediatrician and psychoanalyst who, in the mid-twentieth century, came up with a number of ground-breaking theories concerning early-life development. One of them was the concept of the 'good enough mother', in recognition of the fact motherhood is fundamentally about being able to meet the basic needs of the infant in her care. Everything else is a bonus – therefore don't beat yourself up and pile on more pressure when the job already often feels like you're trying to push water uphill. Here, I'm extrapolating to apply this concept to the role of step-parenthood too. Your 'good enough' job, as step-parents, is to be compassionate, patient, prepared to take responsibility for your own actions, and to care about your impact on your blended family. That's it. Everything else is a bonus.

Take care not to replicate the role of parent

Some step-parents may attempt to replicate the role of parent, but, in most cases, step-parenting is an entirely separate thing, with distinct but subtle differences – which can go unnoticed to those more used to the nuclear structure. For example, you may choose, step-parents, to forego giving a definitive response to an unusual request from the kids, out of respect for their parent – i.e. not wanting to overstep your authority. You may say something along the lines of '*I suspect I know the answer, but let's wait and ask Daddy that question when he comes back!*' Yet to any nuclear family parents within earshot, this may be incorrectly (and frustratingly!) perceived as you passing the buck, or not wanting to be the boundary setter to avoid being thought of as the strict one. This sense of being othered may play out with the nuclear parent picking up on it and saying something like '*Oh I see, you just want to be the fun one – making us all look bad!*' This misinterpretation may be said simply in jest (or not), but it can feel exclusionary, and remind you starkly of your non-parent role, leaving you feeling that you need to justify your actions.

One of the great joys of being a step-parent is you can work with your step-children to create a bond that is unique to you, with its own special ingredients. This may include some of the elements of parental support and care, of course, and will be more readily given and received if the same-sex parent isn't in the picture for any reason – but with a twist that is yours to co-create.

So, you might not be the first port of call to soothe a cut knee or the emotional impact of a mean bully at school, or doing things like attending parents' evenings, choosing schooling solutions, or liaising with medical teams to help them through an illness. Nevertheless, step-parents can certainly enjoy providing an ongoing source of support and reassurance to their step-children, and being looked up to in much the same way as an older family member or godparent might be – someone to have fun with, confide in and learn from. Just don't fall into the trap of trying to double up on a role that already exists, doing both yourself and the kids' parent a disservice in the process. Create your own instead!

Early stage check-ins

By now you're hopefully looking forward to getting stuck into the business of establishing your own blended family. This is the ideal time to check in with yourself and your partner, while the relationship is in its early stages. Here are some things to consider:

- Are you clear about the role they want you to play in their/ your children's lives?
- What role do you want to play in their lives?
- What areas do you think you'll embrace with ease, and are you clear on the ones you think you may struggle with?
- Are you aware of the context of the prior relationship

between your partner and their ex, and how the previous relationship ended? Are there any unhelpful dynamics or circumstances that could impact your relationship and ability to form a strong connection with your partner's kids or them with yours?

One of the challenges of step-parenting is that it is often a thankless task, and step-parents often feel that no matter how much they love their step-children, the fact they're not the children's 'real parent' is never too far from the surface. This may be a source of disappointment, or something you're grateful for, depending on your relationship with your step-kids.

However, an important truth to acknowledge is the significant role you will play in shaping the self-esteem of your step-children – regardless of how frequently you see them. Parents are renowned for loving their children *unconditionally*. A step-parent, however, often plays a role in bringing up their step-children, and so can be influential too (particularly as time passes). Yet, there is no rule that says step-children should or even can be loved *unconditionally* by the step-parent figure, who is arguably close enough to form a distinct view of their step-child's character, but not necessarily close enough to love them in this way. So, as a result, when children aren't loved, liked, valued or respected by their step-parents, said child can, sadly, internalise this as their being truly unlovable.

My step-mother really didn't like me . . . I don't know why. She met me when I was ten. Maybe I was a precocious kid? Maybe she didn't like my personality, or felt I was a threat to her relationship with Dad, or something else – no idea. All I knew is that she made it clear in subtle ways, over a long period of time, that I got in the way. She didn't want me to stay. She discouraged Dad from seeing me and then didn't like it when he saw me without her . . . That sort of thing.

I started thinking that maybe she, without being blinded by biological ties like my parents, was the only one who could see the 'real me' – and maybe that person truly wasn't good enough, likeable or loveable. It made matters worse that Dad never seemed to stick up for me – so, to me, it was like he was saying that how she was treating me was right. So, yeah, I think my self esteem took quite a hit for a while . . . Luckily I found a great therapist when I was at uni, but it definitely took a while to undo the impact this had on me.

Sophie, step-daughter (25)

Sophie's original letter to me, as part of my research for *Step Up*, went into a lot more detail. In it, she described the subtle campaign of psychological and emotional abuse she had endured over the long term. In her case, this was characterised by a lack of empathy for her position, blame and judgement, gatekeeping of the parent/child relationship (where contact is minimised or discouraged in some way by the step-parent), gaslighting (a denial of her reality), as well as a general undermining of her character. While this by no means characterises every step-parent/step-child relationship, it is certainly not an isolated occurence; similar experiences have been reported by many step-children who are part of a mal-adjusted blended family. For example, as you'll read below, Carys' experience in her blended family also greatly affected her self worth, this time as a result of her step-*father's* behaviours.

My mum remarried when I was only three years old. My step-father provided for the household in many ways – Mum felt looked after, and the extra money really helped. However, when Mum wasn't around he would treat me and my older sister badly. Shouting at us both, punishing us severely for small mistakes. We learned to become quiet and submissive around him. Mum wasn't around to see most of it, but as we grew older we learned that the little we did say would not be taken seriously, so it was easier not to say anything – especially as it would upset mum. Eventually they had a baby of their own, a little girl. She was treated like a princess by her father, and, as a consequence, I naturally started to compare myself to her. Believing I must be in the wrong, I learned not to like myself. Today the relationship between us all is much better, but I still don't think I'm good enough.

Carys, step-daughter (36)

Like it or not, step-parents, regardless of your own intentions and behaviours, you're about to take on a role with which lots of people have developed a negative relationship, either through myths that exist in popular culture or their own personal experiences. Yet, without any personal evidence to the contrary – such as Carys' experience of her step-father – the male step figure can often be thought of incredibly positively: welcomed, even. They can be treated as the hero of the family dynamic, and perceived as a sort of saviour, helping to bring together an unstable household, or rescuing an unhappy mother.

Of course, we must acknowledge how step-fathers can also be treated with caution, just like step-mothers. At times we may wonder: is he safe to be around the kids? Does he pose a physical or coercive threat within the family? Will he expect to put his own stamp on the household, dominating the family in the process? Yet, sadly, it is female step-parents who have borne the brunt of suspicion throughout history.

How the 'wicked step-mother' has emerged as a trope in popular culture

Despite often being quietly powerful behind closed doors, for centuries women have been made vulnerable – afforded a lower societal status and less legal protection than their male counterparts, for example, as well as being excluded from particular educational routes and many professions. Add to this travesty the fact that the childbirth mortality rate was historically high, and, due to the practicalities of family life if nothing else, for those widowers desiring to marry again this would have necessitated the search for a new partner. The result was that step-mothers and step-daughters alike were frequently thrust together through remarriage. Often at an emotionally sensitive time, if the death of the biological mother was a thing of the recent past, which often meant they became what we might call survival rivals. Necessarily forced to compete for the affections of the more powerful male figure, they regarded one another from a negative vantage point.

The step-mother was frequently perceived as a threat, someone looming insidiously, prepared to 'steal' what belonged to the daughter – in this case both love and material goods. The step-daughter could also be perceived negatively in turn, getting in the way of the adult relationship, manipulating the father into taking sides and deprioritising his romantic partner.

Both parties were competing for the same prizes, of course – emotional security, financial protection and opportunities for themselves. In the case of the step-mother, instincts to protect any biological children she already had would have only added to the pressure she felt. Campfire stories handed down from generation to generation have consequently stoked a sense of fear and resentment towards women who found themselves in that role.

While the 'evil' step-mother archetype was already present in ancient history – for example in Greek mythology and Roman literature – let's stop and take a quick meander through a more contemporary door, marked 'Brother's Grimm', which may be useful to help us to understand why kids can often struggle to initially accept their step-parent (in particular, a step-mother). This detour will take us briefly into an exploration of our internal relationship with the 'feminine ideal', and the mother archetype.

When compiling and developing new fairy stories, the Grimm brothers, Jacob and Wilhelm, found that their intended juvenile audience were initially incredibly accepting of the step-mother figure. Hurrah! However – plot twist! The brothers recognised that part of being human is that we all have both light and dark within us, and we're all capable of both good and bad. They also knew that children are fascinated by violence, blood and gore, and found it thrilling to read of such gruesome acts. So, keen to include this dark stuff, in early versions of their tales they initially made the mother figure responsible for bad and evil deeds, not the wicked step-mother we're now familiar with. This, understandably, horrified the children.

The kids couldn't stomach the idea that a *mother* figure could commit dark and violent crimes. Their internalised view of the mother archetype was that she could *only* do good – displaying character traits such as warmth, generosity, a softness of spirit and kindness. And so, in response, the Grimms found ways to kill off the mother figure to make way for a step-mother instead, whom they could define as wicked without upsetting their audience. Err, what?! So, now, thanks in part to their literary licence, the step-mother figure has gained all this extra cultural baggage, which has passed through generation after generation.

Over time, and because the stereotype has become baked into the collective psyche, it has become even easier to ascribe negative characteristics and the unhelpful Wicked Step-mother stereotype to any step-mother, precisely because we are *expecting* her to fulfil this role. We even have a name for it – confirmation bias. It's much harder to begin any relationship with a truly unbiased view, and consciously consider the positive characteristics of a new figure, who we may not have chosen, in our lives, so we take the automatic, unconscious – and arguably lazy – route, and judge her.

Let's also consider the role of popular culture and entertainment. Have you ever watched the film *Stepmom* (1998), starring Julia Roberts and Susan Sarandon? Until later in the film, when Sarandon's character is diagnosed with a cancer she eventually succumbs to, Julia Roberts' titular step-mom is ostracised and abused by the kids' biological mother and consequently her prospective step-children, who are resentful about their dad's new serious romantic relationship. And let's not overlook the influence that the likes of Disney have had on our collective psyche when they popularised the Grimms' versions of stories like Cinderella and Snow White. These and subsequent adaptations heavily shaped and influenced the views of our young and most impressionable minds.

Step-mother figures are variously cast as cruel, evil and scheming, and in the case of Cinderella in particular, the step-mother's children – the 'Ugly Sisters' – are portrayed as entirely one-sided characters who don't have a kind bone in their respective bodies. The father figure, meanwhile, is generally passive or invisible in these stories, making it incredibly easy to assign responsibility to the female characters for our big feelings of envy, hate or resentment. We should never under-estimate how these sorts of 'harmless' books and movies can wreak havoc with our psychology and understanding of family dynamics, sowing the seeds for fixed views that develop and reside in our unconscious – well ahead of any personal, direct and *real* experience we might have of a blended family.

Fast forward to today in Western society and what has changed? Well, a great deal. Since the days of Cinderella, we have had women's liberation and the equalising of gender rights on this most basic of fronts, setting the tone for other change. We have since witnessed various political movements, and have changes to gender rights and the revised employment policies of some organisations to thank for a shift towards equal opportunities concerning lifestyle, education and career choices. We also have more relaxed divorce laws, helping to de-stigmatise both the concept of divorce and the blended families that inevitably follow – meaning they too are more readily reported.

The rise of social media and the internet has also raised awareness among and provided resources for blended families across a national audience, and we have more celebrities and influencers than ever before discussing in positive terms their role in their own blended families. Agnostic of social class, blended families exist in all corners of society – indeed, several members of the UK's royal family are now a part of one too.

So while we have a great deal more opportunity to raise our collective consciousness about the benefits and unique complexities that blended families bring, and how to interact healthily with them, it is clear we have come a long way. I would therefore expect the outdated stereotypes we have so far discussed to start to be challenged over the coming decades, as more contemporary and realistic depictions of step-parents continue to emerge. And the more we challenge them *together*, by actively celebrating positive examples and role models, the more we can speed up this evolution.

Changing the story

While we should always be wary of the dangers of stereotyping, we also cannot deny that sometimes, sadly, people's lived experience does indeed live up to popular rhetoric – thinking back to Carys' and Sophie's experiences, for example (pages 27 and 28). On the other hand, I have also spoken with many step-parents who second guess their own behaviour with their step-children on a regular basis, and hold off from standing up for themselves when the children are rude and unkind, or from reinforcing behavioural expectations, for fear of being written off as 'wicked'. So, to help you tell the difference, let's take a closer look at what behaviours are and aren't appropriate, in the context of being a step-parent:

Ten signs of a healthy step-parent

- You genuinely care about your step-children.
- You want to form a good relationship with them, even though it's really hard at times.
- You are encouraging – or supportive of – your partner spending time with their kids.
- You can easily spot your step-children's qualities and strengths.
- You can easily count other areas of your life where you're highly regarded and recognised as dealing with your authority positively, e.g. career, teaching posts, charity works, other childcare responsibilities. How you operate in one role, where you're able to be more dispassionate and less emotionally involved, does not necessarily mean you are also operating as a healthy step-parent! But the purpose of including this is to help you think objectively about the strengths of the various aspects of your broader character, and how, perhaps, your perception of

your own behaviour can be skewed when you step into the role of step-parent.

- You don't take full responsibility for conflict or tension, but you do care, and, as an authority figure in the children's lives, you make an effort to resolve disagreements.
- You recognise the power you have in the dynamic, and actively take care not to abuse it.
- Kids can be infuriating, rude and difficult at times. You recognise this is a normal part of growing up; it doesn't define the kids' characters and you know they're not like this all of the time.
- When they do behave badly, you deal with it appropriately: you're not a doormat or an emotional punch bag. By setting boundaries with your step-children, you help them to manage their behaviour and understand their impact on you – but you do so consistently and in a way that isn't punitive.
- You don't carry grudges.

Ten signs it might be time to work on your step-parent role

- You encourage your partner not to see their child(ren), a sign of the gatekeeping in the relationship that we heard about earlier from Sophie's experience (page 27).
- You're happy when your partner 'chooses' to spend time with you over them.
- You carry strong negative feelings towards the children that you can't quite explain, and don't attempt to do anything about – it's obviously their fault, after all.
- You behave in ways that demonstrate your dislike of your step-children without seeing a more balanced view – you

actively ignore them, consistently bad mouth them to your partner, you withhold kindness from them.

- You consciously prioritise, take the side of, and demonstrate favouritism towards your own children, if you have them, in a way that you're aware makes your step-children feel 'less than'.
- You don't care about setting boundaries with them – you tell them off and punish them, but that's about making you feel better rather than helping them to learn and grow.
- You don't make a sustained effort to build relationships with them.
- You don't attempt to see their point of view when there is conflict.
- You don't take any responsibility for any tension/conflict that exists and neither do you try to resolve it.
- You carry grudges.

The second list is likely to be an uncomfortable read, especially if some of it resonates with you. But if these statements do apply to you in any way, then don't despair. Step-parents can feel isolated and alone, and there are often broader circumstances that will exacerbate an already difficult dynamic – particularly in the earlier days and particularly for the step-mothers among you, for the reasons we looked at earlier. If your partner ignores or refuses to set boundaries with their children, if they don't demonstrate their own respect for you in front of the kids, if the kids act out or are rude to you, if your partner doesn't attempt to call out negative behaviours nor set a boundary with their ex, who maybe criticises you in front of the children, if you are being undermined regularly in front of the children, and so on. Don't buy into the idea that you're the only one who should take responsibility here – most of the time that's far too simplistic.

To help things improve, you can seek individual psychotherapy to help unpick the root causes of your feelings, counselling to help you through a particular crisis or rough patch, and you can seek couples therapy to help talk about the situation together. But don't suffer in silence – things can get better with patience, willingness and sometimes simply the passage of time. The fact you care enough to want to seek a bit of support and take responsibility for whatever your part is in it all says a lot about you and your character.

And, finally, here's a home truth: if you feel you're aligning with the second list most of the time, and you don't feel the above two paragraphs resonate at all, then it might be time to consider your motivations for being in a relationship with someone who has children. Perhaps it's time to rethink what the relationship is giving you. Don't be afraid of moving on – you only get one life and everyone deserves to feel safe, happy and fulfilled.

If you're new to step-parenting, my advice would be to be gentle. Be sensitive and receptive. A little bit like how you'd approach a skittish horse. No sudden movements! Show that you're safe. Also, your relationship with your partner is so important and deserves time and attention, but know that your partner has children. In other words, don't just try and create a relationship of two, at the expense of a family unit that very much includes the children as well as the grownups

Edie, mother and step-mother (45)

The term 'blended family'

The term 'blended' is challenged by some as being too idealistic and out of touch with reality, with the focus instead falling on the difficult aspects of step-families. Yet, I would argue that to aspire for things to get better does not invalidate what can be an incredibly taxing and frustrating reality, nor our need to acknowledge and process these challenging experiences. So we must find a balance between lamenting what can be a grim reality vs living only in the fantasy land of the ideal. Therefore, the term 'blended family' still has lots of value. We may still have a long way to go in terms of our collective understanding of it, our acceptance of it, and its optimisation, but the term still serves its purpose rather than presenting a need to think of new ways to describe the exact same thing.

Names and roles

Which leads us to names and roles. I have heard step-parents variously described initially as a friend, an uncle or auntie figure, a second mum/dad, and, more recently, as a bonus parent. It's important here to acknowledge the advantages, but also the challenges, that these words bring – the labels we ascribe to one another matter.

Firstly, on the face of it, the terminology described above is either neutral or positive, which is good. The words you choose should help the kids to relate to their prospective step-parent, and offer a sort of unspoken blueprint, which speaks to the safety of the step-parent figure; someone who can be trusted.

In the case of the word 'friend', the sort of relationship this intimates has an equal dynamic. The word 'friend' also potentially undermines the fact the primary relationship the step-parent has is with the children's parent not with the child. The expectation of a friendship dynamic also presents a challenge if you're expecting your partner to play a role in influencing and helping to instil behavioural ideals, and set clear boundaries with your children – particularly if they are younger. It may even end up undermining the authority a step-parent figure should have in the home.

I want to be clear here that I'm using the word 'authority' in recognition of the role, and the age and maturity gap, that (generally) exists between step-parents and step-children. In all forms of parent-child relationship, the parent figure (step, adopted, biological or otherwise) is a kind of authority figure. The step-parent will undoubtedly play a role in influencing their step-children's outlook, so asserting their authority in gentle and subtle ways from the get-go will hopefully help set things up for success.

The term 'bonus parent', meanwhile, is a tricky one. It presumes the step-parent will act in a parental capacity, which your partner may not need or expect, especially in the early days. It can also be a difficult word for children to hear, triggering feelings of disloyalty towards their other parent. Plus, the kids may feel they are having to relate to their step-parent, as a relative newcomer to their lives, in a way that is too intimate and familiar in comparison to the strength of their feelings. Plus, does the use of 'bonus parent' mean you need to refer to your step-kids as 'bonus children' – and how does that work if you're childless? Bonus implies extra of another relationship you already enjoy, vs acknowledging distinctions between roles.

Describing a step-parent as an 'auntie' or 'uncle' figure sounds fairly harmless, and, indeed, it may be so – just be mindful of the children's associations with any aunties and uncles already in their lives. If there are negative associations here, and if they are fleeting figures in your children's lives for whatever reason, and that doesn't match the presence your partner will have, then I'd caution against using these terms.

Instead, using first names for step-parent figures from first meetings onwards is entirely appropriate, and allows the children to build a relationship with that person, free from pre-existing connotations of other relationships they might have. It also won't compromise their sense of loyalty to their other parent. When describing your new partner to your kids, you can simply say you have someone special in *your* life that you'd like them to meet – you don't need to name the relationship the *kids* will have with them at this stage.

In some cases, much later down the line, the children may even decide to refer to your partner as Mum or Dad, or their step-siblings as brother/sister, without the prefix of 'step'. This is more likely to happen if the other parent isn't around – in the case of bereavement, for example. Or it may come about naturally to honour the relationship that's developed between step-parent and step-child(ren). But, at all stages, let monikers come from the kids, as opposed to them being something that's imposed by the grownups.

In summary, whatever words you choose will be unique to your circumstances. The golden rules here are:

- Don't prematurely force verbal intimacy on relationships that are too young to have matured.
- Ensure words, labels and descriptions accurately reflect the role your new partner has in your life.
- Take care to ensure the words you use are age and contextually appropriate.

I often get asked, when does a step-parent become a step-parent? My response is often something along the lines of 'there is no right time to introduce that term'. The general consensus suggests this to be a certainty upon marriage. But what about before that? In British culture, at least, we have largely moved away from the view that marriage has exclusive rights to long-term, deep and meaningful relationships. You may have been together for years, have been living with your partner's children for a long time, and you may not be planning to get married at all. So, in these circumstances, it would be entirely appropriate to refer to the relationship between you both using 'step'. Mostly it's a question of state of mind – if it feels acceptable and appropriate within the context of your family dynamic, then allow it to be just that.

> When I was approaching my marriage, I wondered if my soon-to-be-husband's daughter would feel okay if I referred to her as my step-daughter. I decided to approach her and broach the subject – the last thing I wanted was for Cassie to feel awkward in social situations. Unexpectedly, Cassie shared she was surprised that I wasn't already referring to her in this way; she had thought of me as her step-mum for some time already. I was so relieved, and also encouraged that Cassie was so accepting of me. I think it brought us closer together. I even wondered if I should have had the conversation earlier . . .
>
> *Polly, step-mother (42)*

From Polly's experience above we can see that talking things through clears the way for everyone to have their needs met, and these conversations can reveal new information about the depth of the relationship and the comfort levels of those within it.

The prospective step-parent, understandably, can feel incredibly anxious about meeting their partner's children, and the dynamic is loaded with additional cultural and historical complexity, it's true. But over and above all that, the step-parent will also be bringing their own experiences of being part of a family to bear here – from childhood and adulthood, nuclear, blended or otherwise. If this applies to you:

a. **Listen to what your feelings are trying to communicate to you.** Anxiety, for example, is not a bad thing in itself – it's just information that tells us how we relate to something, how much we fear the consequences of a future event or are worried about something we're about to do. In short, one way or another, we often feel apprehensive or anxious about things that matter to us; feeling that way can provide the fuel we need to prepare for something thoroughly. Only when we understand our feelings, and where they've come from, can we begin to do something about them.

b. **Build a library of trusted support sources.** Your partner, first and foremost, should be a source of support – someone to share concerns with and with whom you can work together on how to approach things. Friends are important too – for empathy. A coach, perhaps? – if your focus is to help you practically decide the way forward. A psychotherapist too – to help you understand and work through what you bring to the situation, such as a difficult experience that has left an upsetting emotional scar. A good therapist will also help you clarify how you feel about things you may not have ever needed to consider before, and will help you to find ways to approach the new dynamic healthily.

c. **Every family dynamic is co-created; only take responsibility for what's yours.** Your partner will be bringing just as much baggage to the relationship as you, if not more – we looked at guilt earlier, for example, but in some respects that's just the tip of the emotional and practical icebergs. And, of course, the children will be bringing their own baggage too, depending on their age. Even if they are young, and hopefully so far lacking their own deeply entrenched emotional scars, the chances are pretty high they will express themselves from time to time in a way that will be hard for you to deal with. Plus, for most teens and adolescents, huge hormonal swings will be wreaking havoc in their day-to-day expression regardless of anything else that's going on. So do not take responsibility for more than you need to. It could well be a good idea to proactively see a couples' therapist, who can work with you both to help you consider how you want to approach your new blended family.

Ex-partners/co-parents

Regardless of whether it was their choice to end their former relationship, it's often very hard, excruciatingly so, for a former partner to see their ex move on and build a life that doesn't include them, especially when they share children. That's completely understandable. It becomes even more maddening when separations are bitter and acrimonious – so the ex-partner is not only bruised, but frustrated and maybe even a bit embarassed, knowing their ex is happy and settled with another, particularly before they themselves have met someone new. However, as adults, we get to decide how we behave, and our behaviour is our responsibility. When we hold other people responsible for the feelings we carry, we cause harm to others, stop ourselves moving forward, and become stuck. We can do better for ourselves.

The ex-partner may also then go on to meet someone else who has kids. Now they simultaneously occupy the roles of ex-partner, new partner, parent and step-parent, which can really turn the heat up. Happy and immersed in creating new bonds – and potentially dealing with another ex-partner's upset – while simultaneously healing from and letting go of their former relationship and family structure: it's a lot. It's easy to see how common it is for the feelings of those in blended families to be hugely conflicted as they grapple with several different roles at once.

If you find yourself, regardless of how happy you are in your current relationship, in the position of struggling to deal with the fact your partner has moved on and met someone else who will be a part of your children's lives, consider what you can proactively do to help yourself move forward. The aim is for you to learn to relate to the blended dynamic in a healthier way that affords you some peace.

Don't hold on to grudges, it hurts the kids and stops you from moving on.

When I was newly single after my marriage broke down, I was miserable for ages. If I'm honest, when my ex told me he'd met someone new, I was heartbroken, and I made it as hard as possible for them in the early days. It made it worse that the kids seemed to really like his new partner, so I took every chance I could to chip away in the background, to try and make them turn against her. Pouring my energy into it meant I kept myself feeling down, and wasn't in the right frame of mind to meet anyone new.

The turning point for me was one day, my eldest (who was studying Psychology at uni by this point) said, 'Mum, you're not helping anyone with this attitude – if you met Julia, you'd actually really like her. I get you two are never going to be close friends, but we're tired of hearing negative things about her and

Dad. We all just want you to be happy; why do you need to be so nasty?' It was awful to me that my daughter might not look to me as a role model in this area. So, I decided to get some counselling and gradually realised how destructive I had been. Now I'm in a much better place, and once I'd stopped trying to fight a battle I never had a hope of winning, I found I was much happier anyway. A few months later I met someone else, who treats me brilliantly. I hate to admit it – my current relationship is much better for me than my marriage was, so in some ways I wish we'd separated sooner.

An ex-partner, anonymised at their request

Friends

Outside friendships are actually incredibly important when it comes to forming a new blended family. We rely on them for safety and connection. Whatever role you're in – step-parent, parent, co-parent etc – utilising trusted people around you, people outside the family circle, will likely provide an invaluable source of comfort and support.

Given the number of blended families out there, you'd be hard pressed to not know anyone who has direct or indirect experience of one. So, it's highly possible your friends will have a strong opinion (one way or another!) on what you're sharing with them. You can't control what anyone else thinks or feels, but do take care to ensure they are clear on what you need from them when it comes up. Venting to trusted friends is a really healthy way of letting off steam, clearing the way for more productive conversations with your partner. You may want to raise something sticky with your partner, say, but having really got it out of your system with your trusted confidante first, and heard their perspective, you'll find you now have the headspace to think about how to approach the conversation constructively and sensitively.

Grandparents

The role grandparents have to play in a blended family is frequently overlooked; we often focus instead on the immediate family unit – the kids and the grownups in the parent/step-parent roles. We don't immediately consider the part that the older generations have to play. But why shouldn't we? Grandparents are often heavily involved in their grandchildren's lives, and can make an important contribution to the development of a healthy blended family. They are sources of support for their adult child, who may feel like they're having to start over, or who has met someone with kids.

However, it can be hard for a member of an older generation to accept there is now divorce/separation in their family, as Western society hasn't always been so tolerant about such things. Many cultures *still* don't recognise it as a viable option for broken-down relationships. Religious beliefs may amplify disapproval levels, possibly more so if the bond with their ex-son/daughter-in-law was strong.

Grandparents can also heavily influence the next generation too – both their grandchildren and their child's prospective step-children – for good and for bad. They can bad mouth Mummy/Daddy's new partner subtly or overtly. They can refuse to acknow-ledge their former son-/daughter-in-law, if they have contact through childcare responsibilities. Or, much more constructively, they can choose to remain neutral, or even act as the glue, making the difficult early stages a lot more bearable, through acceptance of their child's new circumstances.

One of the hardest consequences of grandparents lacking acceptance that their children are now part of a blended family is that any prospective step-grandchildren are more likely to feel excluded and rejected. This can be damaging to self-esteem. I heard from one parent who lamented the fact that every year her parents would buy her biological children presents in the holiday season, but would leave her step-children out. This left her feeling awkward, her step-children feeling unwanted, and it caused friction between her and her partner. This scenario could be the result of a number of factors, such as lack of communication, not understanding the impact of such actions on the children, not wanting to compromise on principles, wanting to make it clear the new partner is not accepted, and an unwillingness to embrace the new dynamic – there are several possibilities.

However, it is important that all children in a blended family feel part of it, and therefore, if there is such a thing as an ideal here, we would see grandparents embracing all children in the family – whether biologically related or not.

When our daughter, who has two children of her own, met her new partner, we were so happy she'd met someone she wanted to settle down with – the breakdown of her marriage had hurt her deeply. She then told us he had three children from a previous marriage. We didn't want to be false and jump in too soon, as we already have two grandchildren that we love dearly, but neither did we want to create an awkward atmosphere and have his kids feel left out at birthdays and at Christmas – we tend to make a fuss of the two we have already.

So we decided from the start that if they (our daughter and her new partner) were going to make a go of it, then we'd get to know the kids and love them as our own. We have a great relationship with them today, and our biological grandchildren haven't suffered at all – if anything the fact that we are so close to our step-grandchildren has made it easier for all of them.

Sonya, step-grandparent (75)

2

Understanding Kids

In this chapter we're going to spend some time exploring the mindset of the kids involved, and some considerations you may want to bear in mind, depending on their stage of development.

Tiny ones (0–5)

The needs of infants are all-consuming, so it's easy for parents to de-prioritise their own needs in the early years. The needs of the adult relationship consequently take a back seat, and any issues or dissatisfaction parents do feel is often set aside in order to preserve the family unit. Perhaps chasing an idealised family dream, or a belief that things will get better. Staying out of duty, to 'do what's right for the kids', or a fear of external judgement for leaving a relationship when the children are so small, are some of the factors that point to the likelihood that the number of blended families featuring such a young step-child is likely to be a minority.

However, this can't always be the case, and so, for the sake of completeness, we're starting with what could be the smallest category both in age *and* volume. Little ones don't have a voice of their own, and even if they are old enough to talk, aren't able to understand or articulate their feelings beyond their most basic needs. They certainly aren't equipped to be conscious of or understand the complexities of the adult world.

Babies' inherent vulnerability means that any step-parent figure will be required to take a much more hands-on role. Also, their additional needs and total innocence will mean the adults in their lives will feel a lot more protective towards them. This includes the step-parent, who is likely to quickly become attached to the baby or toddler. There are lots of books on parenting, and so here we'll focus more on the relationship between the adults in the equation.

Some people embark on new relationships where children are involved without a strong desire to have children of their own, it's true. However, regardless of the age of the children involved, common sense and ethical best practice tells us that it would be foolhardy to start a relationship with someone that had children if you weren't willing to embrace them.

However, if babies are part of the dynamic, this best practice is never more relevant. The stress levels associated with parenting a baby or toddler do not disappear simply because we've exchanged the word 'nuclear' for 'blended'. Both members of the couple will need to work very closely together as a team to ensure that the baby/toddler is looked after appropriately during the time they are with you.

If the child is particularly young, the custody arrangements may be biased in the mother's favour (if the baby is being breastfed, for example), but every situation is going to be unique and there may be lots of reasons why the father may be granted majority or full-time custody. Indeed, this may increase in the future, as traditional gender roles and norms evolve. Considering the impact of this on your blended family is important; inevitably co-parents will instinctively be a lot more involved and practically invested in the care of the child at this stage.

Step-parents, if your blended family household has a tiny one within it for all or part of the time, take care to balance your personal attachment to the little one with the sensitivity that is required when looking after someone else's child – particularly, of course, if the co-parent is still in the picture. You will inevitably have a great deal of influence over your step-child(ren); if you have known them since birth or as toddlers, they will grow up knowing you as a significant caregiver, and may become incredibly attached to you. This is an honour and a privilege, and can be immensely emotionally rewarding – but it also brings with it tremendous responsibility.

Responsibility here extends to being sensitive to the parenting style of both households, assuming your step-child lives across the households that each of their parents occupy. As a general rule of thumb, check-in regularly with your partner to ensure you're aligned on what needs to be done. It's also good practice for the couple (as far as possible) to align with the individuals of the other household. This is in order to respect both parents' wishes, but also to aid the healthy development of the baby – the routine will provide stability as they develop.

Parents, you don't need to be reminded, I'm sure, that looking after a small child is no mean feat – and while your partner may love their new role and adjust to it with ease, that can't and won't be the case for everyone. From your perspective, you'll likely welcome an extra pair of hands to help look after your little one, but it's important to find a balance of effort that works for both of you. Understanding and being respectful of your partner's needs during this time – just as you need them to be of yours – will make the world of difference when it comes to relationship and household dynamics. You will need to talk through areas of concern, and think about ways you can help each other out, adjusting styles and patterns to benefit your household.

Co-parents will likely feel a sense of heightened territorial instincts in these early years. From the perspective of the parent who isn't looking after their own children full time, while they may have been ready to end their romantic relationship with their child's parent – or accepting of it, at least – a negative aspect of this process will now mean they see their children less than they would otherwise have done. This period of adjustment in itself can be incredibly challenging emotionally. If this is your reality, over time and as you start to adjust, you may be able to see the advantages of your new lifestyle, which we explore in a little more detail in Chapter Three.

Assuming you don't have safeguarding concerns as far as your ex is concerned, it's important to trust that your co-parent will make a healthy choice with regards their next partner, and to know they would not allow someone they didn't believe would have a positive impact on the child(ren) you share to be so intimately involved in their life. However, just as with any situation (not limited to blended families), if you are genuinely concerned about the welfare of your infant while you are not with them, then there are routes of escalation available to you within the confines of the law and social services.

Little ones (6–12)

Blended families often form once kids are a little older. When the intensive childcare of the earlier years is over, this is often a period of re-evaluation for couples who once were happy but now feel their relationship is no longer working.

From the perspective of our blended families, this is a great age range to introduce kids to someone new, as there is enough neuro-plasticity in their young brains to help them adapt easily to new environments, flexing with relative ease to the needs and norms of different households.

If you both have children, bringing them together around this age is also slightly easier than introducing teens, particularly if you are able to do this before puberty has a chance to kick-in. Defensive psychological structures have yet to harden, and their approach to the world is comparatively open minded vs their older counterparts. We'll discuss intros a little more in Chapter Four.

All kids need and deserve to feel safe in their environments. However, in this age group, with their additional awareness of the world around them, parents will invariably be faced with questions concerning basic elements related to survival – for example, how often will they see Mummy/Daddy, where they will live and how will life work now that their parents have separated. Take care to offer lots of reassurance, helping them to adjust to and accept things more readily.

Kids of this age are also more susceptible to influence, particularly soaking up anything they hear from their parents. Plus, if one of the co-parents is unhappy about the fact the other has moved on, without conscious intervention to balance out their mindset, it's more likely they will attempt to sabotage their children's acceptance of the new relationship. Out of a sense of loyalty, children may side with their upset dad by treating their mum's new partner with disdain, or perceive their dad's new relationship as a threat if their mum is overtly displaying her hurt in the background.

Needless to say, fostering a dynamic where a child is encouraged to act out their parent's anger, sadness or frustration implicitly or explicitly carries the hallmarks of vindictive behaviour, and can backfire. Allowing this behaviour to continue is highly likely to have far-reaching implications for all – it is unhelpful to harbour such negative feelings, and actively unhealthy for a child's developing psyche to learn to approach significant relationships with caution, mistrust or dislike. Plus, sustained behaviours like these can affect the long-term quality of the blended family dynamic, and also the relationship between parent and child. Here, at one end of the spectrum, we can see how the child may feel they need to look after their parent, or become either unhealthily attached to the one they perceive to be the victim, while at the other end of the spectrum, feel frustrated with their victimhood and inability to move on.

So, best practice here, for the sake of everyone's psychological health, is to encourage the new relationships that form as the separated couple move towards creating their own blended families. The ex-partner may well find the new dynamic excruciating, and that's completely normal – but in this case, if this is you, do find ways to deal with your negative feelings, for your own sake as much as for the sake of your children and the broader dynamic. Here are some suggestions:

- Talk it out with a therapist, who will enable you to make sense of your feelings, provide support and validation, or a helpful perspective to help you move on.
- Chat to friends and family members if you want to keep things closer to home. Tailored support groups will also connect you with people going through similar life events.
- If you'd prefer to tackle your feelings alone, consider keeping a journal (incorporating both your conscious thoughts as well as your dreams) or even drawing your feelings in terms of colours and symbols.
- Need to let off steam and deal with the physical toll that stress takes on your mind and body? Then move, in whatever way is available to you. Walking, and gentle forms of exercise like swimming and yoga, can be meditative, stress relieving, and help you to process whatever is trapped inside. Hitting the gym or going for a run will also release endorphins.

Step-parents, remember that approaching your partner's children with kindness and love, and showing interest in their lives and their interests, will pay off in the long run. Remember that strong relationships are not built overnight, particularly if your partner only has infrequent custody of their children.

Teens (13–18)

It probably won't come as much of a surprise to learn that teens are perhaps the most tricky age group when it comes to blended family dynamics! Puberty is in full swing, and hormones cause moods to swing wildly. For even the most typically mild-mannered teen, behaviours during this phase may range from being sullen and withdrawn to hostile and openly rude, and everything in between, as our teens go through a process known as individuating.

Individuation is where the young adult becomes more independent, and begins to identify to a much lesser extent with their parents as a normal part of preparing for adulthood. All of this is typically punctuated with lots of opportunities to re-bond with Mum/Dad, as displays of emotional or practical vulnerabilities unconsciously communicate a need for parenting that remains in spite of all this.

In addition, because of this high degree of internal and psychological development, a teen's ability to rationalise will typically be much more limited than their future adult selves may be able to demonstrate, plus they will generally be more cynical and concerned with their outward-facing image than the more carefree existence that characterised their younger selves. So, all of that – coupled with exam pressures, changes to their rapidly developing bodies, and generally feeling more self-conscious in the world – can create a hotbed of complexity for the prospective blended family to navigate.

I definitely don't have 'all the answers', but I can definitely empathise, being a step-mum to two teenage girls. I have a great relationship with my husband's younger daughter, but the older one is much more . . . difficult. At times she will ignore me, or give me one-word answers to questions – yet at other times she is incredibly close, loving and kind. I look after them with my husband full time; their mum isn't really in the picture. Not having children of my own, and having had a terrible experience with my own step-mother when I was growing up, I struggle sometimes with my step-daughter's behaviour – is this normal teenage stuff, or am I doing a terrible job? I would hate to be unwittingly handing down the same treatment that I received, and I love both my step-daughters. But, yes, sometimes it's a thankless task, it has to be said.

Anne-Marie, step-mother and step-daughter (48)

Anne-Marie's experience above is not uncommon. To help with her situation, and others like it, the couple dynamic needs to be rock solid to deal with the reality of living with a teen, particularly in the early stages of the relationship, as boundaries are still being set, and everyone is adjusting to the new normal. Routine may be hard, and your teen will have a much greater degree of freedom and personal choice when it comes to where they wish to live and how they want to spend time with each parent (and step-parents), in comparison to younger kids.

Factoring in all of this, step-parents will need to be patient and consistent with their behaviour towards step-teens. Kids of all ages need strong boundaries, to help them feel safe and teach them social etiquette. For our teens, strong boundaries more consciously model how they can learn to value themselves as they get older, by becoming self-aware and appreciative of the types of behaviours and dynamics that are good for them – and those that aren't. Boundaries help our teens appreciate others around them too, and help them understand their own impact on their immediate environment, which is vital to maintaining healthy relationships.

It's a little too tempting in a blended family to shy away from setting boundaries with teens. Parents can let feelings of guilt – vis à vis the separation, for example – override this important step. Overcompensating behaviours, such as turning a blind eye to rudeness etc, can replace a stronger, clearer parenting style. It's helpful to remember, however, that teens will behave in this way whether they're in a blended family or part of the nuclear family construct. While, of course, a parental separation is likely to temporarily destabilise their sense of wellbeing and stability, the blended family itself is simply not the cause of difficult teenage behaviours – so overcompensation isn't necessary. In fact, setting boundaries consistently and clearly will help your teen feel safe and benefit them far into the future.

Because they're growing out of childhood, teens typically appreciate honesty and being levelled with. It signals to them that they are more mature, capable of handling more grown-up stuff. However, while adopting this position at all times is sound in principle, I'm sure you can think of lots of examples where it's more appropriate to give young adults a version of the truth that is more palatable for their ears and level of maturity.

Now let's turn to another tricky phenomenon often displayed by our teens in blended families: territorial behaviours. Illustrating this point using gender normative terms, this may include things like young male teens acting protectively towards their mum, or young female teens displaying proprietary behaviours over the dads, in relation to the triangular dynamic that exists between parent, step-child and step-parent. From the perspective of the step-parent, this common dynamic can feel maddening, isolating, exclusionary and unnecessary.

Nonetheless, it's important to acknowledge this for what it is – entirely related to the teen's unconscious drives to practise adult behaviours in relation to those closest to them, establishing themselves as an important or even dominant part of the family hierarchy in the process. If it could be verbalised, said teen might say something along the lines of: *'I'm growing up and I don't want to be actively parented. In fact, sometimes I want to show how well I can look after them [the parent] instead! But I still need my mum/dad and don't want them to forget me, especially now step-mum/step-dad is in the picture.'* This feeling will lessen over time as they mature, and the more you as the grownups help them to feel secure. What all this isn't, is a personal attack on the step-parent, or a conscious desire to erase them from the picture.

Parents, if the behaviour is particularly challenging, however, then to help alleviate hurt, you can step in for a chat with your teen, setting expectations. Providing reassurance and love, you can gently set a boundary that makes your partner's important role in your life and the household clear. You can also find ways to ensure your teen has one-to-one time with you, which at times they will need and crave. This helps them to see that, despite your having a new partner, you will always be their mum/dad and be willing to make time for them when they need you.

Step-parents, you need to know that this stage is not without its upside. The bonding period is fun and exciting; as a step-parent you can largely side-step the intense desire the teen has to individuate away from both Mum and Dad. You can focus instead on role-modelling adult behaviours, acting as a confidante when approached, showing your teen step-child the ropes, as it were.

Speaking of being a confidante . . . This opens another door to a potential minefield that exists with our teens. So far, we've looked at authenticity, boundaries and proprietary behaviours. Let's now turn to the topic of keeping confidences, and how to navigate this while balancing the need to maintain and invest in the couple dynamic. This means respecting your partner's role as the parent, while taking steps to subtly show the rest of the family that the blended couple together form a strong, united and cohesive team. Most importantly, when setting this tone, it's key this relationship is respected by everyone.

We're looking at keeping confidences in this section, as our teens have now moved away from the highly dependent childhood phase, and in experimenting with separating out from Mum and Dad are developing their own identities, which could be the polar opposite to their parents' own lifestyle choices, e.g. clothing preferences, interests and habits. They may not feel comfortable disclosing these differences to either parent – in an effort to retain privacy, or through a fear of their disapproval. In this phase there are also a lot of 'first times'. While parents can be the last people teens want to confide in – often seen as the enemy – step-parents can be given an easier ride. They might be seen as 'cooler', more trendy and worldly, which the teen may want to emulate. So, teens may open up to their step-parent about things that wouldn't reach parental ears.

Step-parents, you may be confided in about serious matters, particularly if your mutual relationship is established. This might include things like taking drugs at a party, or having underage sex with a first boyfriend/girlfriend. It goes without saying that confiding in you at this stage demonstrates a high degree of trust. However, you may wish to signal to your step-teen in situations like this that you're going to need to share this with your partner; as their parent, they have a right to know and will want to be able to look after their teen. You can find a way to gently work with your step-teen to help them find the best way to let their parent know. Perhaps you could offer to share the news, if they are a little apprehensive of how their parent might react – or you could help to facilitate the conversation?

On the other hand, if the information shared with you is harmless enough (e.g. a crush at school, a kiss with said crush – you get the picture . . .), then likely it won't be an issue to keep the confidence, and doing so may build trust and strengthen your bond.

Overall, in order to help this type of dynamic work for all the relationships, it is helpful to have a conversation with your partner. You can discuss together where you would be comfortable keeping the confidence vs when disclosure is necessary.

As your presence in their parent's life becomes established, your step-teens are going to look more closely at the relationship you have with their mum or dad. Teens need stability just as much as younger children, and in addition to feeling secure, by this age they will more consciously be looking to your relationship as a blueprint for how to conduct themselves in their own adult relationships. Regardless of the fact that one of you is not their biological parent, the stronger your relationship, the happier they will be, as a general rule. A desire to trust in the stability of parental relationships unites all family constructs here. The more security you can offer, with fair and clear boundaries, and the more love and kindness you can provide, the greater the chance you have of a calm, happy household and a well-adjusted teenager.

Adult children (18+)

It may seem odd to have a section in 'Understanding Kids' to do with adult children, who are clearly not still children by definition. Yet, the importance of attending to blended family dynamics, and the impact of an unhealthy familial dynamic, does not magically go away simply because someone has turned eighteen. In this dynamic, where both parties are considered to be adults, the adult step-child can begin to decide for themselves how, and to what to degree, they form a bond with their prospective step-parent – just as those step-parents aiming for a healthy and positive relationship with their step-kids will need to put thought and consideration into how they will develop and maintain the bond with their prospective step-children.

Some factors that affect how adult children might behave and adjust to the arrival of a new step-parent include:

- The context of Mum and Dad's separation – what happened, was it amicable, what do the adult children know and from whose perspective was the information shared (i.e. how biased is it?)?
- The context of the parental relationship – how long was it, and what was the quality of the relationship like?
- The mindset of the adult child – are the wounds of parental separation still fresh, or were they healed many years previously?
- Living arrangements. These days it's not uncommon for adult children to live with their parents, due to continued financial dependance, despite being relatively independent in other aspects of their lifestyle, such as self care or fulfilling social needs. Of interest here is whether their living arrangements have changed as a consequence of parental separation. While living with one parent, to what degree are their attitudes towards the other one, and the broader separation, impacted by their parent's mindset and narrative?
- The personal values of the adult children towards the concept of separation and divorce, based on not just personal experience but their learned interpretation of cultural and societal norms.
- The lifestyle and circumstances of the adult children – perhaps they are married by the time you meet them, with families of their own?

These factors impact an adult child's attitude towards Mum/Dad's new relationship to a greater extent than younger children, where the impact is felt on a more emotional level. By adulthood, people are quite capable of having their own thoughts and feelings that exist relatively independently from their parents. To what degree they are expressed and dealt with appropriately, of course, will depend on the health and security of the parent/child relationship. Smaller children can, of course, express their feelings, but their views and opinions are generally bound up in those of their parents, and they won't have the perspective, maturity or ability to process or articulate themselves in the same way as adult children.

When you are first introduced to your adult step-children, you will be able to gauge the 'temperature' by their questions, conversation, body language and tone. To some extent you'll take your cue from that. Here are some things to consider proactively, however, to enable you to step into the new relationship confidently:

- Talk to your partner about what role they would ideally like you to play in their lives. Over time you can work on the reality of this together with your partner's children. As adults themselves, they will have agency, and their views are just as important here – you can't force someone to spend time with you if they are unwilling. But understanding your partner's perspective will give you something to be mindful of.
- Get a heads-up from your partner as to the context surrounding the end of their previous relationship. Forewarned is forearmed!
- Answer their questions honestly.
- Be curious about them in return – look for common ground.
- Allay any concerns they have, which may be implicitly or explicitly communicated. Try to read between the lines, and

encourage an open dialogue, seeking clarity if you feel they are holding back/something isn't being expressed.

- Be patient and don't try to force it; there will be plenty of opportunity to build a relationship organically over time.

If you are an 'adult child', consider the following:

- Try not to preoccupy yourself with the context of your parents' relationship and the fact it has ended. Relationships end for so many reasons, and ultimately if at least one member of the marriage was unhappy with it, and attempts to repair it failed, it's better for both of them to have a chance to be happy and learn and grow with another.
- What relationship does Mum/Dad want you to have with their new partner? Over time you can work on the reality of this together with your parent's partner – as adults you both have agency and the ability to work on your relationship together. Understanding your parent's perspective from the start will give you something to be mindful of when you're introduced to their new partner.
- What relationship do you want to have with them? You can take your cue from how the first few meetings go, but it's good to have a view in advance to help you plan how you ideally wish to behave.

Dealing with negative feelings

As an adult child, try to approach your parent's new partner with an open heart and mind. Your Mum/Dad may be incredibly happy; presumably the relationship makes them feel good and meets their needs. If your feelings towards their choice of partner partly relates to your own sadness/frustration at your parents' separation, guard against holding the new partner responsible for the demise of a relationship that wasn't theirs to invest in or uphold. In the same way as the only people responsible for a marriage are its participants, the only people responsible for its ending are its participants.

If your feelings stem from a protective instinct towards your parent, try to work through what is causing you to feel like this:

- For much older parents who have passed the mid-life stage, you may feel the natural protective instincts that come as they start to age.
- Maybe there is something about their partner that has caused you to feel apprehensive; planting seeds of needing to protect your parent?
- Perhaps you perceive your parent is vulnerable in some way – perhaps they are timid or historically have had unhealthy relationships?

Once you've identified why, take constructive steps to deal with these feelings appropriately. Could you talk to your parent? Would it be appropriate to share these feelings with their partner? Could you seek out therapy and work through what you're bringing to this situation that may not be necessary?

If you are the parent, however, then consider the following:

- Have a chat with your child(ren). Perhaps the relationship has now been established and there's a need to course correct an unhelpful dynamic? Or perhaps it seems to be going really well – great, so far so good – but you may want to check in with them and understand their perspective. Particularly if you are planning to take things to a more serious level with your partner. Definitely check in ahead of a first meeting – do your kids have any initial concerns they can share with you, giving you a chance to reassure them? Are they clear on your feelings for your partner, and intentions for the relationship? How will you position them, the new partner, to your kids?

- Hold the mirror up to yourself: are you doing everything you can to facilitate a healthy relationship between your kid(s) and your partner? Is there anything more you can do?
- Have a chat with your partner: is there anything you can do to facilitate the relationship they have with your kids?

The bottom line for all in each of these scenarios is that quality relationships built for the long term require a) you to understand and take responsibility for what's yours – what I call dealing with your 'emotional suitcases' (more commonly known as baggage!), and b) clear and respectful communication to those around you.

> I value my relationships with all my step-kids and I love speaking with them and spending time with them. They are all special people to me and I am glad to have them in my life. I hear myself telling everyone about their achievements, and seeing them grow from teenagers, when I first met them, to happy settled adults all making their way in the world, is immensely rewarding. I feel like a real father must feel, but without the hassle of early years, sleepless nights and potty training!
>
> *Tom, became a step-father aged 48 (65)*

As Tom shares, if the step relationships began when the kids were still children, by the time they have matured and the kids have reached adulthood, the bonds can be deep and strong – based on mutual appreciation, respect, and a genuine love for one another. As with traditional parent/child relationships, step-parents will naturally adjust their interactions with their step-children to accommodate their life stage and increased maturity.

On the other hand, if the relationship was fractious early on, while it's hard to transform the relationship as the years go by, it's not impossible. Here, step-parents (and adult step-kids, for that matter) can consider re-approaching the relationship and consciously broaching the subject of refreshing the connection, this time getting to know one another as two adults rather than an adult/child. Now the step-child is an adult, their extra agency, maturity and adult perspective means they will be able to respond and adjust to help the relationship blossom – and the step-parent will now, of course, have had many extra years of life experience and should also have a greater maturity than before. Perhaps, step-parents, you might find it easier to relate to your adult step-child in a way that was hard for you when they were younger. Given the lack of genetic connection, step-parents may feel they have more license to attempt to repair challenging relationships in this way with their step-children. Somehow, it feels a bit more natural to do this, compared with say, a traditional parent/child relationship, where the reset/refresh approach may feel a bit contrived.

Step-siblings

Meeting and subsequently building relationships with step-siblings can be hard and challenging, but also immensely rewarding. While researching this book, I was particularly touched by Charlie's experience:

I was one of the children in my blended family. There were already three of us, and then Mum met a guy (Alec) who had two kids of his own. They then went on to have my littlest sister together. So we were a big family, all under one roof right from the start.

After we'd dealt with the niceties and had all been introduced for a while, it's fair to say we got along okay. One day Mum and Alec sat us all down and said that we had two choices. We could either spend time distinguishing between biological sisters/brothers, or we could recognise that we were all equal, all living under one roof, and all part of the same family. They were straightforward like that and we liked the opportunity to think about it for ourselves, that we didn't need to just go along with the status quo. We did away with titles from there on in, and so no one said 'half' this or 'step' that. We were all just brothers and sisters, and to this day we all get along like a house on fire. Twelve years on, I still love being part of such a big family – we all look out for each other. If I ever was in the same position as Mum and Alec, I would say the same thing as they told us all those years ago.

Charlie, part of a blended family (27)

As with so many of the topics we will cover in *Step Up*, we could probably dedicate an entire book just to this subject alone, to properly reflect the broad nature and complex flavour of these relationships. Step-sibling relationships are affected by so many factors, including:

- The quality of relationship each child has with their own parent.
- The attitude the blended couple have when it comes to introducing their respective children, and how much effort they put into helping their kids form bonds and build a relationship with one another.
- Each child's perspective on the separation/divorce of their parents and their acceptance of their parent's partner.
- The parents' respective parenting styles, which the children have become accustomed to, and to what extent they are compatible.
- The relationship they each develop with their step-parent.
- In cases where one half of the blended family move into the other's home to create a blended household, the hierarchy the existing occupants each enjoy relative to the newcomers – as well as the efforts of the incoming step-siblings to make themselves at home.

So what can you do to help step-siblings bond?

- The blended couple are in an ideal position to smooth step-sibling relationships along. It's not going to be plain sailing, so make allowances for teething issues at first as you integrate your children's lives.
- Do everything you can to create a positive atmosphere and opportunities for bonding, so that each child is seen as valued, and attention is shared out equally.

- Don't develop norms that can easily be interpreted as exclusionary. For example, when going on a family holiday, invite all your kids, not just those you live with.
- Even if the kids are now 'adult children', bring them all together well ahead of any big milestone, such as moving in together or marriage. Allow them to build a sense of camaraderie so they can befriend one another and be there to support each other. In the case of remarriage, they will, after all, enjoy a common bond only matched by biological and adopted siblings.
- When smaller children are part of the mix, align on parenting styles, particularly where setting boundaries and setting behavioural expectations is concerned – more on that later.

When done 'right', these relationships can extend the sense of security your children have and teach them many valuable skills they may carry for the rest of their lives.

In summary, regardless of the age of the children in your blended family, keep an eye on what strengths you and your partner can each bring to the table that will help them to develop – even as adults. Avoid creating confusion and division by denigrating the co-parent's parenting style. Instead, while they're with you, focus on creating a secure dynamic that helps to meet their needs, allowing them to learn from you, feel safe, and develop trust.

3

Understanding the Couple

A couple running a blended family deal with lots of complexity right from the start – whether they both have children, or just one of them does. Yet one of the key factors in a successful blended family is to what degree the couple who brought it together are satisfied and united. So, while other chapters deal with the broader family dynamic, this one focuses almost exclusively on the couple themselves, and what might be needed to keep the relationship strong and healthy, before and after children are introduced to the dynamic.

Leaving a significant relationship is inevitably hard. It can be so hard, in fact, that it often takes years for people to finally bite the bullet. Add in children to that equation – with everything it throws up in terms of guilt, fear of losing contact, isolation, letting people down (or being let down), abandoned or rejected depending on your experience – and it's a lot to process, so it can be a while therefore before people recover. Particularly considering the significant practical changes to your lifestyle that inevitably ensue – living arrangements, income and so on.

So when the fog finally clears and someone new comes into your life, someone significant enough for you to feel a spark or connection with, let alone be attracted enough to that it feels possible your life is suddenly going to swim back into technicolour focus, it can feel like you're on top of the world.

Honey, I've got kids

This is where the fun begins! First up is the disclosure that one or both of you has children. This is something to share from the start, needless to say. In Western society, it's almost expected as we get older, and embark on a cohabitation or marriage for at least the second time, that we will have had one or more children from a previous relationship. But there are no guarantees you'll meet someone in the same position, especially if that person is younger than you.

If your partner doesn't immediately and easily accept the fact you have children, it's worth re-evaluating even at that point. Custody arrangements notwithstanding, if the children are minors, it's going to be several years before they are independent. Therefore, the chances are you will want and expect your kids to be a part of your partner's life – i.e. the one you build together – as much as possible over the years.

It's also totally fine if you are the one finding out your partner has children, and you just can't imagine yourself being a step-parent if things develop into something more serious. Not everyone wants children, or is willing to take a role in helping to bring up children who aren't their own. The general consensus is that we only get one life and you deserve to live yours according to your terms. So, if kids aren't for you, then go and live your best child-free existence, and make it count.

But . . . if that is how you feel, and you press ahead anyway – beware! The chances of this not becoming a serious thorn in the side of your relationship if you choose to stay, perhaps in the hope you can convince your partner to spend less time with them, or care less about them, or in the naive hope that it won't be an issue for you, are slim.

So, let's now assume that you're reading this because both you and your partner are happy to accept the presence of each other's children in your own lives.

Prior to meeting the kids

Parents, in the early stages, it's likely you'll wait a while before introducing your children to your partner – we'll go into detail about this in Chapter Four. But earlier on, ahead of introductions being made and the blended family coming together, this is an ideal time to enjoy being part of an adult couple that doesn't yet feature the younger generation.

You'll have access to one another almost exclusively in the time you're together – enjoying adults-only time to begin with. For the one (or both of you) coming out of a previous family dynamic, this can be an exciting time, as you suddenly find you have more child-free time to rediscover the things you used to do before kids.

If you both have children, you may well decide to have more date nights, and slowly get to know each other. Perhaps you're meeting at hotels for snatched weekends away together, or visiting new restaurants you've been keen to try for ages, in the times you are 'off-duty' from your parental responsibilities?

Perhaps you've also been re-discovering your own identity, taking more of an interest in being active, buying that puppy that was off-limits before, or painting the bedroom that shade your ex couldn't stand? This time, where there are clear boundaries marked between time spent enjoying adult/couple activities vs actively parenting your children, can feel incredibly refreshing. You might have spent years rearing young children, perhaps in an increasingly unhappy dynamic, where the main focus was parenting, rather than doing things on your own terms, or investing time and effort into your relationship.

So, with someone new, it might feel like your personal identity has been restored, and the resultant relationship will benefit from a period of relative separation from the burdens of family life.

Now is a great time to focus on enjoyment and getting to know each other, ensuring the foundational boxes are ticked, that you have a strong enough connection, your values align, you feel safe and comfortable, and you can picture your future together. Assuming yes to all of the above, and that you're planning to introduce the children into the mix at some point, it's also time to talk through basic practical details like:

- Future living arrangements.
- Custody arrangements.
- Co-parent (i.e. your/their ex) dynamics.
- Requirements of the children (e.g. are there any behavioural problems or additional needs?).
- The role you might want each other to play as time goes on and the children enter the dynamic.

Plus, unlike a nuclear family where the couple are yet to become parents, or are still bringing children into it, the blended family couple can explore the following subjects too:

- Personality of each of the children and their associated needs.
- Parenting values and skills of the member(s) of the couple who have children.
- Potential prior experience being part of a blended family.

- Desire to become a step-parent and understanding of how you might handle the role.
- Understanding of how your partner has dealt with the serious matter of their separation from their relationship, and possibly the nuclear family. How did they tell the kids? To what extent were the kids considered? How have they approached custody arrangements?

I often hear things like *'I don't want just anyone to meet my kids . . .'* or *'I'll see how my partner handles it when I introduce them . . .'* But I can assure you it's never too early to start talking about these topics, to save heartache later on. Having an eyes-wide-open approach to the creation of your blended family is smart, and one you'll thank each other for later down the line.

Plus, in the interests of equality right from the start, it's just as important for someone who doesn't *already* have children to consider whether their new partner is demonstrating the sort of parenting/ life skills that align with their own, as it is for someone *with* children to be really mindful of who they choose and when they bring that person into their children's lives. Not only might they want their own children one day, but they will potentially have to deal with the negative consequences of their partner's poor choices and parenting style later down the line. If only by virtue of having to watch painfully from the sidelines as your partner parents in a way that you find challenging or unacceptable.

So, remember: just because someone is already a parent, it doesn't mean they wrote the rulebook on parenting, and it certainly doesn't mean they read the same one that you have.

For those couples looking after children most of the time . . .

Once your partner has met your children, however, and has moved in, does this mean you suddenly lose yourselves and the feeling of being a couple? Suddenly when your kids are with you, your partner can be too! And you can be a family together! On the face of it, this is fantastic. But for you and your partner, who may now be accommodating children in the household for the majority of the time, this can present an interesting challenge to your relationship. You're embarking on the next phase of your life together, however, so you may feel a greater degree of security and confidence in the relationship.

Undoubtedly, though, the relationship will be impacted now you can no longer carve out couples time so easily. Even during the times when your kids aren't with you, it's still easy for the main focus to be on domestic chores (washing, ironing, cleaning), as you prepare for the next visit, rather than actively investing in your own needs or your relationship.

So what to do about it?

Firstly, it's important to have regular check-ins. Remember, things can only be considered a problem if at least one member of the couple finds the dynamic tricky. It may be that both of you are ready for the intensity of the relationship to be diluted with domesticity, taking care of the kids and the household. Perhaps this set-up gives you the security you've craved for years – and having been a single parent for a while, or having led a single child-free existence up until now, it might just be that settling into domestic life is exactly what you needed.

However, if, after the relationship has expanded to accommodate active parenting/step-parenting, one or both of you are finding the changes you're having to make too taxing, it's important to talk it through. All the work you've put in so far will now start to pay off. Ideally your relationship is already built on trust and mutual respect – step-parent: you understand your partner's role as a parent is an important part of their life, and parent: you understand it's not an easy task to take on a parenting role for children that are not yours, especially when a co-parent is involved.

Although custody arrangements are not for the step-parent to decide, there is a lot to be said for having equal, majority or full-time custody of the children in a blended family vs a more infrequent arrangement. The more time the kids spend with you, the more quickly the bond will establish, and the more you'll be able to work with your partner to establish the rules and norms of family life together. Although it may feel like a bit of a baptism by fire, once things settle down you should feel a little more empowered and secure, as opposed to a dynamic where the children come to stay infrequently and the house mostly accommodates just you two.

In addition, the two of you as a new couple have presumably come together through choice, and one or both of you will know what it feels like to be part of a dissatisfactory couple dynamic – whether your previous relationship was unfulfilling, making you unhappy, or further up the scale, something you would describe as toxic or abusive. So, for many blended couples, a sense of gratitude and deep appreciation can exist that doesn't necessarily feature in a nuclear or first-time-around set-up.

Unless we consciously work on things, it's all too easy to carry our emotional woundings with us from one relationship to the next. However, new relationships equal new dynamics, which means a fresh start. We may have found a partner this time around with whom we are inherently more compatible, reducing the frequency of treading on each other's emotional landmines. And when they are trodden on, because you're now more self-aware, you're probably better equipped to talk things through rather than fly off the handle – responding vs reacting – having learned from past experiences.

This heightened appreciation and awareness means the blended couple tend to be better at and more committed to looking after and tending to the dynamic they've created so carefully – further increasing the potential for effective communication. Ideally, the new couple raise points of difficulty, navigate through areas of conflict, and demonstrate mutual respect. The early stages of a blended relationship can therefore help our couples feel immensely safe and secure, full of hope and optimism, which has a positive effect on the wider household atmosphere. This gratitude can be a source of real joy for our blended families.

But this new era inevitably won't be without its tricky moments. Now is the time to talk through which bits you are maybe finding challenging. How are they impacting you? And, most importantly, how can the relationship better meet your needs?

For example, your gripes might include:

- You don't have enough 'couple' time.
- You sense that old relationship patterns (either your own or your partner's) are starting to play out unexpectedly and in unhelpful ways.
- You're concerned about areas of your partner's parenting/ step-parenting style.

Potential resolutions may include:

- Finding time for a regular date night.
- Naming the issue you are seeing, describe how it's impacting you and how it may be impacting the wider family dynamic.

Talk about where it might come from, and how you can both work together to nip it in the bud.

- Talk honestly and openly about what you're seeing – do not keep this stuff bottled up. But then balance it out by finding words of appreciation for your partner in the periods when you are both looking after the kids – what *do* you like about their parenting approach, how is the dynamic benefitting your life, what is the new dynamic teaching you and how is it helping you to grow?

If you're both bringing children together, you may find that an additional and challenging aspect of the new arrangement is the discovery that your respective parenting styles/expectations are very different. It's doubly vital here that you pause to talk concerns through before too long, a) for the sake of your relationship – settling on an approach you are both comfortable with will minimise resentment, and b) it's also better for the kids to know that it's one rule for all vs a special restriction just for them that doesn't apply to your partner's children – particularly if they are similar in age.

For those couples looking after children infrequently

Once you've introduced the children, if you're looking after them only infrequently, this will in some ways present an opportunity to preserve and maintain the couple dynamic. Hurrah – you get lots of adult time! But, beware: this way round may also reveal some unexpected bear traps. This dynamic tests even the most compatible couples, and can easily compromise the quality of the parent/child relationship.

1. Disrupting the couple dynamic when the children are there

On the face of it (and depending on your personal perspective), you 'only' have the children for a short amount of time, say two to three days a fortnight. Yet you're so used to it just being the two of you, that you find it harder to get into your rhythm when the kids are there – it's not the norm, so it becomes much harder to adapt to the kids being in the house. This can cause resentment, as (sadly) the children are seen as disrupting the harmony or status quo between you. You may not easily agree on how to spend every other weekend when the kids stay. Or it may cause a big bone of contention when you realise you can't go on a two-week holiday together – not without your partner and their children having to go several weeks without seeing one another. In the process, your mental health will decline, your partner may become resentful, and the children will suffer, which isn't fair on them.

The kids, for however much of the time they're in your house, deserve to feel safe and welcomed. Children can feel easily pushed out when they see one of their parents and their partner only infrequently. I fully accept that at times children read into situations that simply aren't there, but in order to advocate here for the kids in a blended dynamic, I have to say I've heard of some frankly shocking examples in my time, i.e. instances of children being distinctly *unwelcomed* in a blended household.

> In my blended family, my father and step-mother had a baby together. I love my half-brother, but it was so hurtful to see how his needs seemed to be prioritised over and above mine. They would go on holiday and not invite me . . . I was discouraged from staying over, and the few times I was allowed to stay

> with them, I was asked to make-up and strip my bed and bring my own towels. I was obviously a burden and truly felt like an unwelcome guest. The worst of it was seeing the huge pile of presents my half-brother got at times like Christmas or birthdays. I would watch him open them and have maybe one or two things to open, which was pretty hurtful. It's not about the money, but it was clear who was the favourite. I felt like a second-class citizen.
>
> *Finlay, step-son (31)*

It's not easy to hear things like Finlay's story above, so imagine how difficult it must have been for him to experience the reality. From talking to him, it's clear that dealing with this sort of unhealthy dynamic hugely affected him at the time, and it's taken a toll on his self-esteem and the degree to which he feels he belongs in the world, which has carried through into adulthood.

In the interests of balance, we know that the children in a blended dynamic do often act out – typical examples being them giving others the silent treatment, hearing the age-old *'you're not my mum/dad'* being hurled across a room, threats of going to live with the other parent when arguments erupt, or refusal to communicate with a step-parent who's trying to do their best . . . All of these can and do occur, and not infrequently. Any variation of this kind of behaviour can be extremely testing to even the most laid-back of characters, especially when step-parents often feel they don't have the right to challenge this sort of ill treatment.

When children are only living in the blended family household for a minority of the time, undoubtedly it's harder for the couple to get into a domestic routine or family life with shorter visits. These brief visits are often treated as 'quality' or 'treat' time, and if the step-parent figure is new(ish) on the scene, the children may find it hard to adjust to a 'third wheel' always being there – i.e. *'I only see Dad once a fortnight, so I want some proper time just the two of us'.* This can leave the step-parent feeling rejected. It may then be harder to instil boundaries, or get the kids into regular behavioural/activity routines. Though I'm sure we can feel empathy for both the child and adult positions in this scenario.

Minority custody means it will take much longer to foster a deep and intimate connection between step-children and step-parent. This means the onus will be more on the parent to do a lot of the heavy lifting, until everyone adjusts to the new normal – which is tricky, as the parent spending less time with their kids is often reluctant to actively parent: *'I just want them to have a good time with me, why waste time with anything else?'*

What might help smooth things along?

- Parents: ensure the children have some one-to-one time with you as part of every visit.
- Plan activities to do as a group to help develop the bond.
- Parents: talk to the kids about the special place your partner has in your life, reassuring them you love and care for them, your children, just the same as you always did.
- If the kids act out by being hostile or rude, talk to them about the impact of their behaviour. Not just once or twice, but every time. If you turn a blind eye, the message they will receive will be that it's okay to behave in such a way. Is that what you want?
- Both members of the couple: provide support and reassurance to your partner if they find the earlier stages difficult.
- Step-parents: spend a little time with the kids one-to-one during their visits too, to help build the relationship between you. This

is a delicate balance and not one to be forced, however. If neither you or the kids are receptive to this it doesn't mean never, it just means now is not the right time. Be patient.

2. Impact of different parenting styles between each co-parent

This will be more obvious the less time you spend around the children. It makes for a very challenging dynamic if you and your partner, in addition to dealing with the emotional impact of the parental separation on the children, are also trying to set boundaries or course correct challenging behavioural norms during the short time they're with you that they're not learning elsewhere. If this is an issue, here are a couple of options to try:

a. Adopting the mindset of 'your house, your rules'. This is a quick and easy way of setting your own expectations, while taking care not to criticise the way that the co-parent likes to do things. It's simple for the children to understand, and particularly effective with younger kids.

OR

b. If the children are old enough, and you'd prefer a more collaborative style, you could open up a conversation with the kids to talk through areas of difference, and understand why they are behaving in a certain way. You can also understand from them what domestic jobs they're expected to do in their other home – you may even be surprised to hear that they're expected to contribute more, and in ways you hadn't even thought of. Aligning approaches where there are easy wins like this can be an unexpected bonus. Don't fall into the trap of doing things differently just for the sake of it.

OR

   c. You could take a hybrid approach. There's nothing wrong with reverting back to the '*nevertheless, we do things differently in this house*' narrative once you've had a collaborative discussion. The key difference with this route is you'll be spending a bit more time explaining to the kids, and hearing their perspective, rather than the more directive approach of Option A.

However you tackle it, ensure you align first with your partner, and endeavour to have these conversations jointly – especially if you both live together. Finally, ensure the step-parent is fully empowered to reinforce the expectations if the parent isn't around. Assuming neither of you is abusing the authoritative power you have, as the adults in the household, this fact deserves to be respected.

3. Difficult feelings arising in the parent

Parents can feel utterly powerless when having to deal with challenging behavioural norms set and reinforced by their co-parent – they're harder to unpick when the kids are only with them for a short period of time. If this is you, then you should know that feelings of frustration and possibly anger at your former partner are pretty common. Try not to let them overtake you, though. You are still one half of the co-parenting team – and as such will always have the ability to greatly influence and impact your kids' values, and their understanding of how to treat the world around them.

Step-parents, if this applies to your partner, encourage them to open up. There's nothing quite like feeling you have a teammate who sees and understands you. Just be aware that while their gripes might be centred around, say, Jack's inability to make his bed in the morning, or Mia's inability to keep her room tidy, often the root cause of someone's hurt lies far beneath the surface.

For example, underneath it all, your partner may feel out of control, helpless, or like their connection with their children isn't as strong as they'd want. If that's the case, try to gently work towards having a slightly deeper conversation, to help your partner understand what's going on, giving them an opportunity to share with you. Once they have awareness, they'll be better equipped to deal with their feelings constructively.

By tackling the situation as a team, and digging a little deeper to uncover the true source of your partner's frustration, together you will also be able to identify solutions that may have a greater impact than just Jack remembering to make his bed in the morning, or Mia tidying up after herself. Although, let's be honest – that would be a great start!

4. Difficult feelings arising in the step-parent

The step-parent may also feel awful in this situation. Picture the scene: Jack has refused to make his bed for what seems like the hundredth time. It's not like he can't, or doesn't know that it's important when he's living with you. But he won't listen to his parent – and he's made it clear he's not going to listen to you, his step-parent. Trying to brush this off is likely to be pretty hard. In fact, you might be thinking: AAAAAGGGGGHHHHH.

This is normal . . . but remember that things aren't going to be just as you'd like them to be from day one. So, how best to handle it there and then? Do you:

a. Gather yourself, count to ten and walk away – you might as well make his bed when the visit is over, and in fact you can clean the whole room at that point too.

b. Signal to Jack that you're a little frustrated at the fact his bed is unmade, and let him know you will need to have more of a conversation about it.

c. Do your best to sit Jack down there and then – surely there's a way to make him understand?

Any of the above options are available to you – and considering this is just one small decision, choosing any of them in isolation isn't going to ruin what could be a very positive relationship in the long term.

Depending on how well you know Jack, any of the above options might be appropriate in your personal circumstances. Option A might give you a way to achieve the goal of a tidy room without 'sweating the small stuff'. And with Option C at least you'd be sharing your frustrations and reminding him of his responsibilities.

But based on what we know in the example we're talking through, I'm going to guide you to consider Option B as a generic fail safe. Remember the kids are only with you for a minority of the time in this example. Plus, you're still figuring out how to balance couple life with one that very much includes the kids. So a degree of treading carefully is needed, certainly until everything gets into the kind of rhythm and routine we can start to enjoy in the more established dynamics we discuss later on.

So, with this in mind, let's think about the downsides to Options A and C. With Option A, you're essentially sending Jack the message that negative behaviour has no consequences, and you're doing nothing to correct it. Plus, you're likely to be left carrying a whole range of difficult feelings that will cause you resentment/irritation/stress (delete as appropriate) if not dealt with healthily. Sure, the room will be tidy – but by your hand and not Jack's. So nothing has changed, and Jack may well be frustrated you've been into his private space while he's not there.

The downside to Option C is that you're leaving yourself, as the step-parent, no time to calm down, reflect, and rationally consider the best way forward. You're also not going to be operating from a position of strength if you fly off the handle and the conversation gets oh-so-helpfully 'reported back' to your partner via Jack – this may inadvertently cause your partner to turn into 'Captain Rescuer', putting you into the position of aggressor and so subsequently chastised in order to protect Jack, in his role as victim (more on this later). Aside from being deeply unhelpful to you, this won't help your relationship with your partner, which is of paramount importance here. And it won't help your relationship with Jack either, who, by the way, still won't be inclined to make his bed!

So considering these points, then, Option B becomes attractive. It's generally a good idea to have a conversation with your partner first, so you can align in the case of sticky situations like this. Remember, this section assumes you have minority custody, and if their parent is struggling to keep the boundary, it's unlikely you're going to have enough influence to achieve the task of getting the bed made, as well as building a positive relationship with Jack.

Sit down and discuss together:

- What is the boundary you both want to set; are you both agreed on it?
- Do you have any insight as to the root cause of Jack's behaviour? If so, it will help to inform the conversation you're about to have with Jack.
- How do you want to communicate your expectations to Jack; what do you need to say?

- Are you going to have the conversation as a joint team, or in this case is it more appropriate that your partner (Jack's parent) has a solo conversation with him? This will depend on the nature of your relationship with Jack, your broader role in his life and your relationship with him (frustrations about unmade beds aside). Ultimately, it's important to focus on the route you believe will achieve what you're setting out to achieve.

Here is an example of the conversation framework you might have with him:

- What's the expected behaviour?
- Why is it important?
- Are there other children in the household that already make their own beds, i.e. Jack's siblings, or your own kids? (A reminder here that you expect everyone to follow the same rules would be helpful, if so).
- What are the consequences if Jack continues not to make his bed?
- Regardless of whether you decide the conversation with Jack should include the step-parent figure in addition to his parent, do ensure that Jack is clear at the end of it that the boundary is to be upheld in the future, and that both adults in the household are going to expect it and will reinforce it if it's not met.

The important thing is that the couple are in this together, and having the children living with you behaving well will only help the harmony between you both, as well as the kids' overall development. So, don't forget you can and should provide support to one another in the background, through listening as well as offering empathy and support.

Let's turn to Naomi's real life experience here, which highlights a common step-parent frustration:

My husband is so conflict avoidant he practically wakes up carrying a white flag. While that sounds great on paper, I actually find it really hard, as when my step-kids (one boy, one girl) behave badly, or are high on sugar or whatever it is, it is often left to me to try and manage things. Sometimes this causes friction between us, as he still carries so much guilt as a result of his marriage ending that he thinks the kids shouldn't be parented with a 'strict hand' – but I think differently. Isn't the job of a parent to help kids understand how to and how not to behave? And if this stuff isn't addressed when it's small, what's going to happen when they're older and too big to be admonished or coached? Plus, if I end up saying nothing then I feel so full of resentment.

Naomi, step-mother (37)

I feel for Naomi here. She wants to avoid hurting her partner or being thought of as punitive, yet she feels strongly that the children need some clear boundaries from time to time, which is a reasonable position. By talking to her partner, though, Naomi is in danger of being perceived as questioning his parenting style, particularly when one of the root causes of the conflict avoidant behaviour is down to the guilty feelings he is carrying. I would still advise Naomi to have the conversation, but with extra tact and sensitivity – thinking through the 'how' and the 'when' will be important considerations here. It may be a relief for her partner to know he has a strong and boundaried voice in the household, but the ideal here would be for him to develop the confidence to step in and pick up the parenting reins a bit more often. Not only would this approach help her to feel a bit more supported, but it would also work to ensure the dynamic is equalised between the couple.

I think Henry's advice, below, really sums it up:

When the children are young, e.g. toddlers, I suppose it's easier for the incoming adult to do some of the parenting once the relationship is established, but it would be much harder to do when the kids are teens. For me, in our household, it was important, as my partner came to live with us, that she help out with this stuff – but in an appropriate way. So, for example, rather than 'tell the kids off', per se, she took the role of reinforcing the behaviours that I had already set, through saying things like 'If your daddy was here and not me, would you still be doing that?'

That approach helped me out, and was good for us as a joint team. Plus, it also gave her some influence over the kids, without her jumping in and reprimanding them – which wouldn't have gone down well. But the truth is, I can't always be around, so I'd rather her tell the kids off from time to time to help them learn how to behave, rather than them learn it's okay to behave badly.

Henry, father in a blended family (43)

4

Making Introductions

In this chapter we're going to spend some time on the practical realities and questions that arise from bringing the incoming step-parent and the children together for the first time.

Incoming step-parents may be thinking:

- Will they like me?
- How should I behave?
- What if they're rude to me?
- How affectionate should I be with my partner?
- What should I wear?
- What should we talk about?

If you're the parent, meanwhile, you may be thinking:

- How do I know this is the right time for them to meet?
- How can I make the meeting run as smoothly as possible?
- I really want them all to get on, but what if they don't?
- What can I do in advance to prepare the kids?

And if you've both got kids, not only will you be managing your own thoughts and feelings about taking this important step, but you'll also doubtless be considering how to manage the children's first interactions with one another.

Meeting the children

Some notes for step-parents
(Parents, this might be useful to you too)

As the incoming step-parent, you'll be wondering whether the children will like you. I'm here to tell you that there's no straightforward answer to that. It will depend on everything from how the groundwork has been laid by your partner, the children's ages, to how the narrative has unfolded concerning your arrival in their mummy or daddy's lives. Assuming they're aware the meeting is to take place, and they understand the significance of it, the children themselves will be managing a whole host of different emotions, maybe without even realising it. They may feel excitement at the prospect of meeting someone new, worry as to how their other parent may feel, contentment that Mum/Dad has moved on and found someone new, concern that they might not be liked by this new partner, and much more besides . . .

However the first meeting goes, remember: **the children's response is not personal to you**. How can it be, when they haven't got to know you? Any negative behaviour will be about what you *represent to them*, not who you are personally. Thinking through some of the more negative projections, you may represent the person 'taking their parent away from them', the person who has 'broken up the marriage/relationship', the person responsible for making the remaining parent 'left behind' unhappy etc. It is natural to want to be liked and appreciated, so take heart and remind yourself that this will come with time. With patience, resilience and consistency – three vital qualities for all step-parents – you will find the relationship will blossom over time. However, you will, of course, want to make the best possible impression on them regardless, to help the initial meeting go as smoothly as possible.

What to wear

Yes, let's start with clothing. This may seem like a trivial point, but choosing the right outfit can be key to feeling confident and primed for an important event – your clothes reflect your personality, and help you prepare for the task ahead. Let yourself be guided by the practical reality of how you're going to be spending the time, and consider the impression you want to create in this all-important initial meeting. Are you going for lunch? Are you booked onto an activity? The more comfortable you feel, the more likely it is you'll be able to relax.

If you're looking for a little food for thought, then start with something relatable, accessible and easy to wear, which can adapt to unexpected situations, such as little ones asking you to play with their Lego or to join in with a game they've made up. If you're looking for some specific guidance, then for daytime meetings consider jeans, smart trainers or boots, and a shirt or fitted top. Perhaps avoid particularly tight/provocative/revealing clothing, as for meetings with infants or particularly young kids this might not be practical, while for older kids it might give them an unhelpful initial impression of you.

How to behave

This will be influenced by how old they are. You'll want to keep your wits about you, and adjust your style accordingly to meet their needs as far as possible. Are they quiet? Talkative? Inquisitive? Boisterous? Playful? Sullen? Friendly? Hostile?

Some good rules of thumb include:

- Be patient.
- Ask appropriate questions that are relatively neutral – for example, about hobbies, school, interests. Nothing too probing or controversial, though. Keep it as light and breezy as you can.
- Try to find some common ground – for example, if you're all doing an activity you also personally enjoy, or did a lot of as a child, why not tell them that?
- Take it at their pace and don't rush them.

Describing your relationship

Unity with your partner is always going to be mega important, and never more so than now. Take the time to have a chat beforehand and decide any topics that might be better kept 'off-limits'. Have a consistent view between you as to how you will be positioned – a 'friend', a girlfriend/boyfriend, someone special that Mum/Dad likes to spend time with etc. Perhaps think of some questions that might arise and try to think of what answers you're both going to be comfortable with.

Younger kids

Younger kids are likely to be more accepting of what you say, but if you're going to describe your relationship as a friendship, then make sure your body language aligns with this – children are naturally observant and known for their intuition.

Teens and young adults

Teens and young adults are likely to ask a lot more questions and perhaps won't take your initial responses for granted. They may be coming to the meeting with an agenda, based on their perception of their parents' separation, or their loyalty to their other parent.

So, work with your partner here, and take their lead if appropriate. If questions are addressed to you directly, try to keep your answers as honest as you can, without feeling obliged to share any detail that you're not comfortable with. Remember you're simply in a loving relationship with a person who means a lot to you. Inherently this is a good thing and is to be celebrated – you are not on trial!

Interacting with your partner

What about your interaction with your own partner? Okay, so if you've followed the advice above, you'll have had, or be about to have, a conversation with them to understand how they would like to play things. Add on to that agenda how you should behave towards each other. Is hand holding okay? Hugging? Kissing?

Ultimately, the answers to these questions are for you and your partner to decide; how you behave with one another will depend on many different factors. For example, if you're a highly tactile couple, then you may want to dial it down during initial meet-ups, allowing everyone time to get comfortable with your relationship, as well as with you. When you have got to know the kids, you may instinctively feel that any affectionate displays are likely to be received positively. If in any doubt, keep in mind these two basic principles:

- In the early stages, less is always more.
- The meeting should be about getting to know each other, rather than treating the kids to the sight of a PDA between you both. At this stage they're getting to know who you are, and the safer and more comfortable they feel around you, the more accepting they'll be of you together.

Avoid the bear traps

All of these dynamics are pretty loaded, so it's easy to fall into common bear traps before you've had the chance to settle comfortably into the new rhythm. Being aware of what might crop up in advance, and how that might be detrimental to a healthy and relaxed environment, will pay off as connections start to deepen.

For example, when it comes to the co-parent (the ex-partner), it is absolutely crucial that neither of you, especially you as the newcomer into their lives, are in any way negative about them. No matter what the child says, no matter how badly you perceive how they may have treated your partner, no matter what your partner says, for you, as the prospective step-parent, this is an off-limits topic. You may not have met your partner's ex before, and so your impressions of them are only down to what your partner has shared, what they see or experience, what anecdotes have been recounted. This will only ever be part of the picture.

When you don't have direct, personal and in-depth knowledge of someone's character, you can only ever understand a relatively narrow aspect of them that has been filtered through someone else's lens – in therapy terms, this is called a subjective reality. Which also, by the way, reflects how your new partner wants you to see their ex-partner. For example, by casting their ex partner in a negative light, they may be unconsciously asking you to collude with them by eliciting sympathy from you. Or perhaps they are looking to be seen as the 'good' parent, by virtue of their own reasonable behaviour, which just so happens to be in stark contrast to their ex's, by way of a 'helpful' comparison.

So, falling into the bear trap of casting judgement is unwise on many levels, and could have multiple unintended consequences. At the very least it may hurt the kids' feelings, and cause them to shut down or become resentful towards you. And at worst it may cause significant damage and affect your chances of a strong and healthy relationship with them. Your aim is to be perceived as either positive or neutral – and remember the old saying, if you can't think of anything nice to say, then don't say anything at all!

Empathise, empathise, empathise

Before we go any further, let's look for a way to better empathise with the kids. Don't forget that while this meeting is a Big Deal for you, it will be for them too. They will feel so many different emotions, and as we touched on above, many of them are likely to be conflicting (happiness, excitement, guilt, curiosity and resentment, to name just a few). And, of course, they're only human. They may not be the model of polite behaviour at first, but they will have their reasons, so try to be considerate.

Kids don't have the luxury of being the adult, at the risk of stating the obvious. Aside from the fact their brains are still developing, they may still be grieving the parental separation, and they have no control over who their parent chooses to have a relationship with. They may well also feel a sense of loyalty to their other parent – or even feel caught between the two. All of these thoughts are entirely normal for children meeting Mum or Dad's new partner for the first time. And if they're particularly young, unlike you they can't choose where or when they are meeting you – or leave if it all goes badly! So remember two of the crucial qualities outlined above: be super patient and as resilient as possible.

Difficult behaviour

Okay, next up: what if they're rude? If this is what you're thinking now, I want you to notice your feelings, which may include a little anxiety or concern. Try not to get too caught up in these feelings; they show this meeting matters to you, which is a good thing. Nevertheless, it's important to remember you can't control how other people behave. What's more, your worst fantasy about how they may behave may be very far from the reality.

Rudeness can be a defensive behaviour (especially if this is a first or second meeting), and often it's a child's way of trying to set boundaries, express themselves or feel safe in a new and unfamiliar dynamic. Consider what role the rudeness might be playing – for example, it might be about trying to hide some of the difficult feelings we've already named. Perhaps insecurity, a lack of safety, a sense of guilt and so on. Keep in mind, too, that you are NOT the parent. In the beginning, don't try to chastise them, and try to catch your own inclination to respond with your own defensive behaviours – like snapping at them, for example.

While, especially in the early stages, the parent is the go-to person for managing behavioural issues, and instilling values, etiquette norms and expectations, there is a difference between 'parenting' and boundary setting, which is important in any relationship. Where any unkind comments or attacks are aimed directly at you, it is okay to be assertive and respond gently, in a way that makes it clear that although you understand this may be difficult, what's just been said has hurt your feelings. You may want to talk to your partner about addressing it, but these things often unfold very quickly and without warning. To diplomatically tackle direct attacks or outbursts and nip them in the bud, here are some tactics to consider:

#1   For younger kids – keep things nice and simple:
A simple 'ouch, that wasn't nice to hear, my poor feelings!' might be enough to show a young child you have been hurt by what's been said.

#2   For older kids – be clear and to the point:
Adolescents and teens may be able to deal with slightly more sophisticated language – 'I get you're feeling X, and that's okay . . . this is a new dynamic for us both, isn't it? It will take a little time to get to know each other'.

#3   For all ages, sometimes it's important to lean in vs avoid

As above, one way to deal with negative behaviours is to lean in. For example, you may be faced with several pointed comparisons to their other parent, which you may sense, through tone/facial expressions or words used, are designed to antagonise you. It's hard to know for sure, but regardless, rather than steer clear of the topic or rise to the bait, try to respond positively or encouragingly, showing interest – you might already know this disarming tactic as 'killing it with kindness'. As well as showing you won't get rattled easily, it will signal that you genuinely welcome them talking about *both* their parents – helping them to feel more secure and relaxed, as a result of you modelling some very secure and healthy behaviour. This approach should serve you well over time, particularly if you are consistent.

Whichever of the options above feel right to you, the underlying win here is that by naming and addressing what might be lying underneath, you will demonstrate you understand the dynamics. That you're aware what is said, often in frustration or anger, or notably passively, is far from the true picture. Most importantly, it shows you're willing to talk about feelings, creating healthy opportunities for constructive conversations.

Once addressed, though, it's important to try to move on, returning to the calm, kind and patient approach you arrived with.

Despite all the potential pitfalls, chances are that the first few meetings will pass by smoothly, as everyone is on their 'best behaviour', trying to make a good impression. Difficult feelings often start to be more actively expressed within a few months of the initial meeting, once the kids start to feel more comfortable, or realise you're here to stay.

Some notes for parents
(Step-parents, you may find some useful nuggets here too)

There is never a perfect time to introduce your new partner to your kids; each new blended family will time things slightly differently. The bottom line, however, is that it's important to give yourself plenty of time to consider the health of your new relationship. If you have any sense that it's not a long-term prospect and you're not sure you see a future in it, it's okay to wait or hold off taking this step. But if you're reading this, the chances are you're feeling settled together, and want to take things further.

As a broad consideration, remember your role, as parent, is vitally important here. The step-parent, as I shall reiterate throughout this book, is often scapegoated and vilified unnecessarily as the blended family comes together. I have lost count of the number of times I have witnessed a similar narrative playing out. As the central figure, however, and the reason your children and your partner are meeting at all, you have a *key* role to play here in helping to minimise the chance of this happening. Underestimate it at your blended family's peril!

In my blended family, my husband set the tone and expectations from the beginning, and we followed suit. He expected me to be respected by his children and his ex partner – who he was co-parenting closely with – and included me in things from the start. At the same time, he expected his children to be respected by me, and made it clear how important to him they were. So we all knew where we stood, and things were much easier as a result.

Andrea, mother and step-mother (51)

Now, on to the practical details. You're going to want to take some time to consider the children's needs and developmental state – their age, to what degree they are settled, and their current mental health more broadly. Do also take some time to imagine how they will respond to being introduced to your new partner. Are they likely to adjust quickly? In many cases, a 'little and often' approach is more conducive to building solid foundations, which may provide some food for thought in terms of how frequently to meet in the early days, as well as the best location to meet. The relatively safe neutral environment of a café or playground, for example, may mean things are more relaxed than the emotionally charged setting of the home, where the children are likely to be used to letting their guard down.

Step aside for five

Suggestions on where to meet

4–7 yrs – a playground plus milkshake kind of scenario may help the children to relax in a safe and fun environment, and give you and your partner a chance to bond with the children in a light-hearted way. The time afterwards at the café provides an opportunity for casual conversation.

8–11 yrs – a group activity goes down well. Try something to focus your attention and make room for conversation, such as a pottery/paint experience, or an escape room.

12–15 yrs – spending time in the same space, while giving the kids an appropriate opportunity for a little downtime to pause and reflect, may be the best approach. Try the cinema, for example, again followed up with some food to create some time for conversation. If you would prefer something more active, consider another age-appropriate activity that will inject some fun, such as go-karting, an experience like Go Ape, or a theme park.

16–18yrs – older teens approaching young adulthood will have more maturity, and will therefore be able to manage their emotions a little better than much younger children. Perhaps create a relaxed opportunity to introduce your new partner in the home environment. Perhaps you could cook lunch for everyone, and if the children are interested in cooking, allow them to take a role in the prep? This will empower them and give them a sense of what it's like to host, with the added benefit of subtly helping them to feel secure and responsible during such an important occasion.

When my kids met my partner, they were fifteen and seventeen respectively. For me, when planning that first meeting, it was about respecting everyone's time, and creating an environment for everyone to meet that wasn't too formal for the kids. I wanted them to feel engaged, comfortable and relaxed. So, I invited my girlfriend over to have a coffee, then we all took the dog out for a walk. Like most teens, my kids are glued to their devices, so a dog walk allowed everyone to be present and make light conversation – nothing too deep! Then we went back to the house and I cooked, while the kids decompressed in their rooms for a while. By the time we got to lunch we picked up on earlier conversations and everyone felt a bit more relaxed.

Robert, parent (55)

Of course you really want the meeting to go well, but as we've already started to explore, there may be all sorts of dynamics at play that may mean you're all feeling a little apprehensive at first. So it's important to ensure you and your partner align together well ahead of the meeting. Talk through your respective expectations, hopes and fears. What do you need from each other? How can you support one another? By attending to the needs of the adults in the equation

– which means you and your partner, working together to hear and understand one another's point of view on all the various elements of this topic – you will both be in a good position to iron out issues that arise during the meeting itself. As the kid's parent, you're naturally going to have a strong voice in the meeting planning, but it's key to work together on this right from the start, to ensure you both feel respected, improving the chances of things going smoothly.

Tackling specific questions head on

Your kids will, at any given time, ask unexpected questions that will catch you off guard. I've heard it all . . . Do you sleep in the same bed? Do you love your new girlfriend more than Mummy? Are you going to marry her? Are you planning on moving him in? Do you love him more than me? What happens if he doesn't like me? And so on. So, it's best to be prepared rather than surprised out of the blue.

A big one that comes up repeatedly is a desire to know how long you've been together – so let's take a closer look at that one. You may have been together for some time, road testing your compatibility and adjusting to life together first before the kids are introduced into the dynamic. There is no problem with this, but keep in mind how this information may be received by the children.

It's not uncommon for children whose parents have separated to have a heightened sensitivity to the idea they are excluded from the parental/adult world. Knowing scary things happen in the hidden world of adults, things which affect them, they may wonder, without saying anything at all: what is not being said? What's really true? Is my world about to up-end again, and can I really trust what's in front of me?

To try to alleviate the kids' sense of 'not knowing', and

uncomfortable feelings, you might notice they become a bit more observant – we call this 'hyper vigilance'. Being hyper vigilant can result in a *lot* of questions! If you think this might be what's going on with your child, it's a good idea to regularly check-in, particularly if you notice them withdrawing, or seeming a bit preoccupied. Remind them that they're safe, loved, and you will always look after and protect them. And the presence of your partner in your lives means extra care, support, love and fun – not something to be wary of.

So while there isn't and can't be a gold standard 'one size fits all' response here, do be consistent, and, generally speaking, as transparent as possible with your messaging. I say 'generally speaking', as you need to keep an eye on practical realities, and bear in mind the ages of the children, ensuring what you have to say is appropriate for their ears.

Make sure you talk with your children ahead of the meeting and answer any questions they may have, again taking into account their ages and adjusting your responses to match their maturity levels. It's important to settle the whole dynamic as far as possible ahead of time. You achieve this by clearing any concerns, and allaying fears through the creation of a safe space where they can open up, talk and express themselves. By doing this, you will role model that healthy communication is an important part of the whole blended family dynamic they are about to be a part of.

Notes for you both if you each have children

Where there are two sets of kids, you may want to introduce them all at the same time – especially if they're all of a similar age. Older children, who may be away at university, for example, may not mind meeting separately, but in that case the meetings should happen close together so that relationships can all develop at a similar pace. The danger in handling meetings separately is that children can feel excluded/less important than other siblings, or the 'other' kids.

Joint meetings aren't without their complexity, however. Not only are you considering the relationship between you and your prospective step-children, but you will also be dealing with your partner's introduction to your own children. Finally, you will have to carefully negotiate the introductions of your respective children to one another.

So, there's a lot to contend with here, and it's not an undertaking for the faint hearted! It's perfectly possible to do this smoothly and well, of course, but you need to remember the three key qualities of patience, resilience and consistency, and add into the mix a high degree of conscious planning, geared towards a united outcome with your partner.

The pre-agreed scenario planning we talked about will become even more important, as you will now have to consider your different parenting styles. If you go out for lunch, for example, and would not normally allow your children to have dessert, but your partner's children are used to tucking into ice-cream, you may want to adopt a consistent approach for the whole family unit.

After the initial meeting – notes for both of you

Afterwards, it may be helpful for both of you to take some time to reflect individually. Block out some time to see your therapist, to journal, or to call your friends to talk it through. Overall, meeting your prospective step-children, or introducing your children to your new partner, is a big milestone, and no matter how it went, you should be proud of yourself for taking that step. Give yourself a pat on the back and plan in a little treat or a reward to recognise your efforts.

Self-care is one of the first rules of successful blended family-ing – how on earth can you be expected to be there for other people if you can't be kind to yourself?!

After that, come together to debrief. If it hasn't gone as well as planned, talk through why, and come up with some ways to improve things. Support each other if you are carrying any disappointment or frustration. Also keep in mind that things are going to improve. The first meeting is just one opportunity, but you will have hundreds more to clarify expectations, work with difficulties as they arise, and reshape and influence the dynamics you both want to co-create.

On the other hand, it's not uncommon for there to be a 'honeymoon' period at the start, where the children associate meeting your partner with fun activities and trips, special meals and treats. During this period, often the mood is light and breezy.

In both instances, good and bad, recognise it's early days, and things may change, but that's okay. Families take time to bond and unify; it takes time for a common language to emerge, punctuated with 'in-jokes', shared experiences and memories, which we'll come to a little later.

You may want to chat to your children now too. How are they feeling? What happened from their perspective? Explore their responses to meeting your new partner, and encourage them to speak freely, allowing them space to open up – only then can you address any fears and concerns.

Take care to contain any strong emotional reaction you might be carrying about the introduction, and how their responses are affecting you. Instead, take these to a trusted confidante to work through, which might be the safety of your partner but might not. This process is hard, though, and the more that you can be there for each other, the stronger your bond will be.

For now, try to notice the dynamic without getting too caught up in the emotional after effects. You've got the first meeting in the bag, and the final part of this stage of the journey is to visualise how you want the next one to go. Where will it be held, how will it progress, what would you like the outcome to be etc?

Planning and debriefing on each meeting is a healthy habit for you and your partner to get into, especially in the early stages. It will help build your self-awareness and manage the dynamic in order to minimise sticky situations. Try not to get caught in the negative thought pattern of 'this will never change, this is just how it's always going to be', though, or worry too much if what was a very positive early set of introductions starts to become a little harder after the novelty has worn off, and relationships start to build and deepen. You are only just getting started – and most importantly – you got this!

If the kids are about to be introduced, should your ex meet your new partner?

I'm often asked whether the step-parent and your co-parent should be introduced, and to what extent it's important they have a good relationship. There are those who would say guard against it. There are others who would say you should do it as soon as the relationship becomes serious. And as ever with so many conflicting opinions, the bottom line is that the only people who can truly judge this are the blended couple themselves – every circumstance is completely different.

So let's have a look together at some of the considerations. For the purposes of keeping things as simple as possible, the next few paragraphs are addressed to the parent who may be considering whether to introduce their now co-parent to their new partner. You are the one with the communication channel to both, and so often you're the key decision maker, likely to be aware of everyone's view first hand.

The fact there are children in the mix can often give people pause for thought – otherwise, typically we wouldn't even consider introducing our ex to our new partner. But it's a very stressful dynamic to manage for many reasons, and should not be considered a given, by any stretch.

When thinking through what's right in your case, have a think about things like: Do both parties (your partner and your ex) actually want to meet one another? If not, then consider very carefully as to why it's come up now as a choice point. What's your perspective? For whose benefit should they meet? You don't need your ex to approve your choice of partner, after all, and if you think highly enough of your new partner to want to introduce your kids to them, the assumption is that you believe they will be a safe and positive influence.

Parents, things may well become tricky if you suspect your co-parent is still emotionally attached to you. Tactile gestures towards you in front of your new partner, reminiscing overtly about old times, 'accidentally' calling you by their old pet name for you in front of your new partner, or displaying 'mock' hurt/frustration if these behaviours are not reciprocated . . . These are all hallmarks of someone who may well be still feeling attached to you, or who is keen to remind your new partner of the once prime position they played in your life. So, for the peace and wellbeing of your partner, as well as your ex (and not to mention your own) – don't feel you need to squash this new dimension into your family's life, if not enough time has passed for both you and your ex to have left your old dynamic truly in the past.

Give blended families some space

Blended families also need time and space to come together and form their own bonds, norms and rituals. The process of developing the blended family can take longer, and become even more complex than it otherwise would be if the 'old' and 'new' adult relationships are also blended from the early stages. It can be very confusing for the children, i.e. *'If Mummy and Daddy get along so well, then why on earth did they separate? Clearly Mum's new partner is just getting in the way of them getting back together!'*

Children, of course, deserve to have a positive and healthy relationship with each of their parents. However, it's entirely possible for children to feel safe and well adjusted in a blended family dynamic, without the grownups all needing to have their own relationships with one another.

Make the decision on your own terms

Even if they meet, there's no need for your ex and your partner to become friends (unless they want to, of course); there's a big difference between being acquainted with someone and becoming close to them. So, if you would feel more comfortable keeping your relationship to a purely co-parenting one, then do just that. The point is, you should not feel under pressure either way.

Family milestones involving both parents and their partners

Sometimes there might be a practical milestone coming up that means meeting beforehand is a very sensible idea to help smooth things along. Often the event is related to the children, who may want both their parents and step-parents to attend their special occasions. The guest list for weddings, big birthdays and even family funerals can all cause headaches for our blended families where there is friction behind the scenes. For it to work, plans must be carefully thought through in advance for the sake of the bride and groom, or birthday girl or boy etc.

Parents: let's say that a large family occasion is coming up, and your partner and your ex are invited. Neither have met before, and you want to ensure the dynamic on the day is as smooth as possible. So a smaller meeting ahead of time may be entirely appropriate to put everyone at ease and break the ice. There might be some collective discomfort about this idea, however, but perhaps this is one of those occasions where short-term pain delivers long-term gain.

Err . . . Isn't all this a bit overcomplicated?

In short . . . no! This is simply part of the reality of what it means to be part of a blended family, and the good thing is that the vast majority of issues are completely surmountable, providing they are thought through carefully. The adults in the dynamic all have a responsibility to look after and protect their own feelings, but also to be mindful and respectful of the broader dynamic.

Where people take a 'let's wing it' approach, there are often very real consequences that can cause a great deal of pain and upset – often for those who are not directly involved.

The following real life experiences illustrate this point nicely:

When I got married, I was given a clear choice: invite Mum or Dad, but not both together. Can you imagine how that felt? It was devastating. If they are separated, all children love for their parents to get on with one another – or at least to be civil.

Sarah, step-daughter and step-mother

When I turned thirty, I held a big party. Dad refused to go if Mum wanted to take her long-term partner. Honestly. Nothing made me feel more like an adult than having to both mediate between and parent my own parents. I was pretty upset but what can you do?

Max, step-son

My brother got married last year. I was expecting someone to cause a scene. I mean, it's a wedding. In the end my step-mum, who my brother and I struggle to have a relationship with at the best of times, got wildly drunk and decided to cause a huge row, in which she got physical for one awful moment. I was just so embarrassed and absolutely furious, and what made it worse was the fact my father refused to step in to try and manage the situation. Yes, we're adults, but the hostility was so unnecessary, and I would have thought Dad would have wanted to protect us, even now. We no longer speak to her as a result, and out of loyalty to her, our father now sadly keeps his distance too. I wouldn't dream of ruining my step-children's big days like that – I never want someone to experience what I have had to go through.

Alex, step-daughter and step-mother

These experiences above demonstrate how adult children of blended families are forced to make difficult decisions every day when drawing up guest lists for their milestone events, to compensate for badly behaved and/or poorly adjusted parents. They try to protect the feelings of the other parent who may have found it difficult to accept their ex has moved on . . . to avoid warring parents on the day . . . or to avoid step-parents/parents bumping into one another. Similarly, even when invitations are extended to all, it's not uncommon for parents to decline them, to avoid perceived conflict with an ex-partner or the difficulty of bumping into their new one. This can be devastating for the adult child, who is then left to pick up the pieces. It can create uncomfortable ripples in extended families too, which is a shame, as most of the time it's entirely avoidable with just a little – you guessed it – self-awareness and appropriate responsibility taking!

Psychological safety

If you are all happy enough for the meeting to go ahead, how can you ensure it feels psychologically safe? Has enough time passed since the ending of the previous relationship for your ex-partner to feel relaxed and neutral at the least, if not happy for you? Do they accept you have moved on and are part of a dynamic that makes you happy? Remember, over 90% of our communication is non-verbal, and people who are upset, stressed or carrying any form of resentment will find countless ways – subtle and not so subtle – of making their difficult feelings clear to the subject of those thoughts and feelings. Often, these difficult feelings can be expressed between the ex-partner and the step-parent (either one way or two ways) – not because they have a personal relationship with one another, but because of what they may *represent* to one another.

113

It may also feel safer to direct difficult feelings towards the step-parent in an attempt to preserve the co-parenting relationship. So, the step-parent once again ends up in the role of scapegoat, taking the brunt of any negativity. Alternatively, the parent about to introduce their children to their new partner can start to feel caught in the middle.

The bottom line

If one of you is uncomfortable with the idea of these two worlds converging, then explore why, for the sake of understanding, rather than trying to force your personal agenda; this is a recipe for resentment and hurt. Your loyalties lie with one another at this stage, and there is no rule that dictates that a meeting/relationship is mandatory. If things have settled down and it feels natural and comfortable in your dynamic, then that's great; there are many instances where ex-partners and step-parents develop positive and healthy relationships, which can even outlive the blended couple relationship. There are also times, as we looked at above, where meeting one another may be entirely appropriate and practical, and may very much help to manage people's feelings and the overall dynamic, particularly in the case of upcoming events. Ideally, though, ensure everyone in the dynamic is either neutral or genuinely happy to be in each other's lives.

5

What Happens When Things Get Serious: The Firsts

Important milestones can lay the foundations for bonds that last a lifetime – it's an uplifting, future-focused time for our blended family, especially for our couple. The first few may not seem like hugely significant events, at least at the time, but within each nevertheless await potential bear traps that can be avoided – read on to find out how.

Staying over

I've separated out just the act of staying over with sleeping in the same bed as another. The purpose of this is to ease everyone into a more familiar/intimate dynamic, by taking it gradually. Whether you choose to do this in two stages in reality will mainly depend on the age of the children.

Staying over might seem like a very normal thing to do, and for couples who don't have children to consider, this may happen pretty early on. However, for the children part of the embryonic blended family, this will signify things are serious.

Assuming the step-parent has built a good enough rapport with the kids that staying over feels like a natural next step, the kids might be excited – and reluctant to go to bed! You'll probably know from direct or personal experience that anything novel that deviates from the usual routine is always cause for a bit of bedtime acting out. If the couple have got this far, this is likely part of a broader intention to integrate with the children on an ongoing basis. Generally speaking, two clear routes open up:

1. Turn it into a fun event. You position it like a sleepover, with special food or a takeaway, a film and some popcorn. Associating you/your partner staying over with something fun will help the kids to view this positively.
2. Keep things low key. Here, you might position the staying over as an act of convenience (e.g. *'Sarah is staying the night tonight because she's got an important meeting in the same town as the one we live in, tomorrow, and her house is miles away'*) or perhaps time it with a significant event, such as a party (e.g. *'Sarah is going to stay over because we're all going to have a few drinks at the party, and it will finish too late for her to get home at a sensible time'*).

Take a moment to consider what feels right for you and why. Or, maybe you've got some ideas that will work even better for your family? How you approach this will be down to your unique circumstances.

Taking it slowly is particularly important if there are older children in the mix who lack the maturity of older teens but have far more awareness than toddlers or younger children. For you as the couple, it can even present an opportunity to have some fun by sneaking into each other's rooms at night when everyone is asleep!

The point is, while you may be putting extra care and consideration into how you start to integrate the family, at all stages there is a way to make it work *for the couple*. Remember to have some fun along the way; you're not martyrs, you're a couple who love each other and are only taking things slowly and cautiously to help the children adjust. Little acts of love to show your care and appreciation for one another when the kids are elsewhere in the house will also help to bond you both – you're in this together!

Do keep in mind that it's not just the staying over to consider, it's the waking up too. So, before your partner – let's use Sarah again, to illustrate the point – stays over, and assuming you're not going to be sharing a bed, have a chat with her beforehand. Depending on their ages, are the kids likely to burst in in the morning to jump on Sarah?

I'm talking to all the potential 'Sarahs' reading this now, but if this is a real possibility, then have you considered what clothes you're going to be wearing? You need to sleep and be comfortable, for sure – but you also may need to be child-proof the next morning . . .

When everyone gets up in the morning, is it clear where Sarah is going to take a shower and get dressed, in a way that protects her modesty and also recognises that, right now, she's a guest of the household?

Then, consider the breakfast routine – an act of familiarity and intimacy for most families, and maybe on weekends everyone eats in their pyjamas. But this may feel a little too intimate the first time Sarah stays over. Depending on when the children's parents separated, it might not have been that long since the nuclear family were all doing this together. And your co-parent may not have moved on and found a new partner yet, so this may be the first time the kids have experienced this. You can't underestimate how important it is to pay attention to the little details for these 'firsts', so everyone feels as comfortable and relaxed as possible.

I became a step-father in my mid-forties. Amelia and I decided we needed to take things fairly slowly and see how things worked out. I didn't move in with her, nor did I spend any nights at her house for some months. Amelia would drive over and spend the evening with me once or twice a week. I would spend weekend days at her house helping out with some DIY and generally making myself useful, but no overnight stays yet. I think that period helped to create in the minds of the kids the realisation that I could be a useful person to have around, if nothing else.

James, step-father (75)

Sharing a bed

Not all couples share beds, and some are perfectly happy not to. But, assuming your preference is to sleep together, then sharing a bed is a step-up in your relationship in the kids' eyes, signalling intimacy. The right time to do this may come down to your intuition and experience so far – how well have the children adjusted to Sarah staying the night, for example? How old are they? Are they wondering why you aren't sharing a bed yet? What do you, as the couple, both want? If you've been sleeping in separate beds for a while when the children are around, then you may be very much ready to take the next logical step.

When the time comes, you could broach this in a low-key way – Sarah is now going to be having a sleepover with Mummy/Daddy. Or, you could time it with an event. For example, if you have guests staying (perhaps during a holiday period), then Sarah moving into your bedroom for a 'grown-up' sleepover to save space might logically move things on and be easily understood and accepted.

Depending on their ages, the kids might be used to coming into the room at night if something is wrong, or they need something. So, another person sharing Mummy or Daddy's bed might not only be confusing, but also a bit off-putting. From your little person's perspective, they may worry:

- Am I allowed to still go in?
- Do I want to go in? Maybe I'll be embarrassed?
- What if I wake up Sarah?
- What if Sarah is cross with me for waking her up?
- What if Mummy/Daddy is cross with me for waking Sarah up?

All of these concerns are pretty common and normal for older children (around 6–11 yrs) to experience, to varying degrees. If you've been together for a while, sharing a bed is unlikely to present any major issues, particularly if the children have a good relationship with your partner. But it's certainly worth explaining your boundaries around this on the occasions Sarah does stay over, if you have children who tend to pop in for comfort and reassurance during the night.

Ideally, the children will be reassured by you that if they need you as their parent, they are free to come in. First and foremost, if your children are of the age that they need you during the night, that has to be the priority. But you know your children and will know if the behaviour is usual or not. Because of this fact, you'll also be able to assess if you see a change from their typical pattern once your partner stays over. Perhaps they start to make a habit of coming in, whereas before they were sleeping through the night, for example? In this case, consider having a chat with them during the day – maybe they have underlying worries they haven't yet voiced?

Going on holiday

Holidays are another exciting step. By the time you're ready to do this, sharing beds will be the norm (unless, of course, you generally sleep in separate rooms and don't plan to share in the future). Holidays are meant to be fun times to bond as a group, and relax from the stresses of everyday life. So, don't make life harder for yourself than it needs to be by a) going too soon, when the group hasn't yet formed cohesively or b) tiptoeing around your partner while you're there – for example, by not showing one another any affection around the kids.

So, for this to happen, we're going to assume that some core conditions are met:

- The children accept Mum/Dad's new partner.
- The group has bonded successfully, given the time they've been around one another.
- Everyone's willing to take this next step.

If you've both decided to take the children away, then firstly have a chat together to decide what sort of trip you think will be fun for everyone, that will meet the needs of the whole family. Nuclear families have lots of the same considerations to think about, but the blended family couple may want to be extra sensitive here. You may need to consider how to handle some of the unique complexities faced by the blended family:

- **Location.** Deciding to go where the kid's parents went on their honeymoon likely won't make for a relaxed dynamic. Consider a destination where everyone can make new memories together.
- **Companions.** Do you take a friend for the children? As a first-time trip for your blended family, you might want to use the

time to bond as a family unit. This is a golden opportunity for you all to get to know each other, after all. But, if your child is an only child, and they are generally fairly extroverted, then a friend might balance out the dynamic. Two kids/two adults also gives you and your partner an opportunity for some grown-up time.

• **Leave no one behind.** If you both have children, unless there's a good reason not to, taking both sets of kids away at the same time is a great idea. You will no doubt want to avoid treating one group differently from the other, and bringing the whole unit together for these key bonding moments will give everyone a chance to adjust.

After you've talked together about the sort of holiday you want to go on, at this point involve the children. Let's say you've decided on a beach holiday. Shortlisting a few options and asking the kids for their opinion is a great way to manage the decision, so that everyone has a voice and a chance to input from the start. Something as small as this can set the tone nicely for the kind of healthy, collaborative family dynamic you want to build.

Then, once plans are made, start to talk about the holiday when you're all together. Think about what activities you might want to do while there. Discussing what routines you all get up to typically when you're away will quite likely go down well, and start to pour positive energy into the upcoming shared experience you're about to have. 'How other people pack' is always a fun topic to get into when you go away for the first time. For example, are you a throw-it-all-in-and-hope-for-the-best kind of a person, or a pack-two-weeks-in-advance-with-a-detailed-list-and-range-of-different-sub-bags 'smart packer' type? Talking about these little details is a fun and easy way to bond and get excited.

Once on holiday, a further range of unique considerations will open up:

- **Sleeping arrangements.** The first time younger children go away without both Mummy *and* Daddy, they have a lot to adjust to. Consider whether they need their own space (not just the normal increased need for privacy that comes with growing up), but to deal with any difficult feelings that might arise as they adjust to the fact that Mum or Dad isn't there, and Mum/Dad's new partner *is* there.
  - o OR, perhaps younger children might prefer to share the same space, even if they have their own rooms at home? Not only might this give them a feeling of safety and comfort, but it might give our blended couple a little more time to themselves once the kids are asleep/in bed.
- **Space.** If the children are young enough not to have their own phones, the parent will be responsible for managing communication between them and your co-parent – consider how you will facilitate this:
  - o Aligning with your usual routine when the kids are with you, you'll likely want the children to have time to talk to Mum/Dad when you're away. But maybe you're all sharing a hotel room or apartment, and privacy is at a premium?
  - o Consider how you'll facilitate chats with Mum/Dad without compromising the privacy of your current partner, or causing unnecessary feelings of upset, envy or sadness in your co-parent.
  - o This can easily happen, e.g. if young kids are video calling Mum or Dad, and in their excitement they decide to show them around your accommodation.
  - o It may be hard for your co-parent to see your partner's

personal items littered around the room. It may be hard for your new partner too – suddenly your co-parent is 'in the room' chatting to their kids, in an intimate setting where it's hard not to overhear – a stark reminder of one of the many clear distinctions between parent and step-parent.

- Parents have a real responsibility to manage the dynamic carefully in times like this to make it as easy as possible for everyone.

Keep talking to your partner as the trip gets underway. There will be so many little things that take you by surprise that even the best-laid plans may not account for. The more you turn to one another for ideas and encouragement, the easier it will be to manage all the inevitable twists and turns – and the more fun you'll end up having along the way.

Above all – don't send any postcards! Live in the moment as much as possible and enjoy this special time.

Moving in

So you're sharing a bed, you've sailed through the first holiday, and now you're thinking of taking the plunge and moving in with one another. Congratulations! We can't cover every eventuality to suit every circumstance – never mind its own chapter, that would need its own book – but we'll focus on two common scenarios:

1. Step-parent figure has no children of their own and is moving in with the parent and step-children
2. Parent and children are moving in with step-parent figure, who has no other children

First, I wanted to share Jenna and Tom's experience of a different scenario – buying a house together rather than moving into one another's space. I was touched by the level of care they had put into their decision:

> We decided to buy a house, so together Jenna and I worked out what part of town and how we would arrange the finances. One restriction we put on ourselves was to keep the kids in their existing schools, minimising disruption to their lives at a time of family change. I knew we would all have to make adjustments, but perhaps me more than anyone – I was the interloper and I accepted that. I was bringing no family of my own to the party, so it was up to me to fit into established family relationships, as well as work together to create our own way of living as a family.
>
> *Tom, became a step-father aged 48 (65)*

I liked the fact that Tom, being in his own words 'the interloper', was keen to build a family life in a way that worked for him as well as Jenna – but not at any cost. It's a good example of the extra considerations blended families have to make that go unnoticed until you're faced with the situation in real life.

NB: Where the children don't live with the couple for the majority of the time, I would suggest turning back to Chapter Three: Understanding the Couple for a bit of an insight here. In the scenario where both members of the couple are bringing children together to live under one roof, I'd suggest turning to Chapters Eight and Nine, where we talk a little more about this phenomenon.

Right, time to delve into the scenarios . . .

Scenario #1: *Step-parent figure has no children of their own and is moving in with their partner and step-children*

If you're the step-parent:

When you move in with someone, it's not hard not to feel, on the one hand, excited and content, but, on the other, a little apprehensive. By now you'll have accumulated a lot of your own *stuff*, regardless of your current living circumstances.

Apprehension can stem from a feeling of stepping into someone *else's* space. This, of course, happens in 'first time around' couple scenarios too, but in this instance, you're not only moving in with your partner, there's an established family group living full or part time in the household. It's easy to wonder: *'Do I just need to fit in with the norms of their household now? How well can I adapt to their way of living? Sure, there's not much room for me, but it's to be expected, I'm moving in with them, it's their territory.'*

If this is how you're feeling, remember two things:

1. You're not alone – this is a well-trodden path. Your feelings of apprehension are entirely justified and all part of the process.
2. Regardless of who lives where, you are choosing to uproot your life, begin afresh with the person you love, and their children. Which means you both have a say in how things are run.

You also deserve space for you as an individual – in the same way you will want to invest plenty of time and effort into building the group/family dynamic: the whole reason you've moved in in the first place.

Take some time to understand the way things are currently done, and if you feel neutral or positive about existing routines, there's no harm in going with the flow and adapting to the current status quo. Like when trying on a new outfit, you may find the 'new normal' fits really well, and in fact really suits how you like to live.

If there are areas that don't quite chime with your own values or preferred lifestyle, however, take some time to understand why. Is this something you can or want to change or alter? Part of – not all, but part of – this chapter for you is about compromise and adaptation.

However, if you still feel strongly, take some time to talk to your partner about how you feel. Maybe you need some more space for your things, or a piece of furniture you have had for decades means so much to you that you'd like to move it in? You might like to take on more of an active role – cooking, for example, or taking some more responsibility for childcare.

On the other hand, maybe you feel you've been expected to take on too much? Maybe your job means that, try as you might, you simply don't have the capacity to take on all the cooking for a family of five, when only a few months ago it was just you to consider? Perhaps you need an evening a week to yourself, or you don't want to compromise on your daily pre-work run.

The point is: don't be afraid to voice your needs. Remember you're moving in with the person you love, and they should want to help you settle in. In an ideal world they'll welcome your ideas and want to respect the boundaries that are important to you. You can always adjust things later on too, if you find some of the changes you have gone along with or instigated simply aren't working. The beauty of a blended family is that everyone has some idea of a family blueprint they were familiar with and would like to emulate in the current set-up – so use it as an opportunity to experiment and see what works for everyone.

If you're the parent:

If your partner is about to move in with you and your children, you're just as likely to be feeling a complicated mix of emotions as they are. Beyond the usual hope, excitement or satisfaction that comes with this sort of change/increased commitment, you may well be carrying a set of fears – *'Things have been okay so far, but staying over a few nights a week is different to living together . . . isn't it?'* Or *'What if the kids, who have seemed so well adjusted so far, suddenly can't cope with this next level arrangement, and begin to act out?'* If this is you, your feelings are also entirely normal and justified – it's a big step to have someone move into what you've come to regard as *your space, your sanctuary,* so you may well feel territorial over it, especially if it's the first home you've made since your relationship with your co-parent ended.

So, just like your partner, you would also be well served by identifying any areas you're struggling with, and doing a little bit of solo work, to try to understand what's going on for you. Do you have reason to be fearful, perhaps based on your past experiences? What work can you do to manage your own expectations, such as coaching yourself to be more patient before forming hard opinions? Do confide in your partner here, giving them the chance to alleviate your worries, or at the very least to hear and understand you.

After your partner has moved in, things will have changed, and previously unforeseen dynamics may start to emerge. These might be very positive, but if your concerns are based on the reality that the changes are impacting the family in negative ways, it's important to sit and talk with your partner, share your concerns and work jointly on ways to improve them.

In addition, as the parent, as well as the partner to someone you care deeply about, you're now wearing multiple hats in your household, and your new responsibilities now include a little bit of brokering. In reality, this might look like actively helping everyone to adjust, facilitating healthy conversations with the kids as well as your partner, or encouraging everyone to take responsibility for themselves and keep an open mind.

Scenario #2: Parent and their children are moving in with step-parent figure, who has no other children

If you're the step-parent:

In the first scenario, we acknowledged your partner might be carrying some feelings of apprehension related to the fact their territory was about to be shared with another. In the second, we can see how you may now resonate with these feelings given the shoe is now on the other foot.

What's more, your home is about to be shared by not just your adult partner, but also their children. You may have a strong and close bond with the kids, but even if this is the case, multiple people moving into *your* space won't be without its challenges. While the move may be for the greater good, and something you're both excited about, do not underestimate the changes to the mood and energy of the house, the impact of new people living in the space, all sharing its resources. There will be a significant change to the dynamics in the house, as well as the routines of family members.

You'll be considering what adjustments may need to be made, e.g. do extra bedrooms need to be created or decorated, or proofed to keep much younger children safe? Practical needs such as these can be resolved by the couple, but as the home owner/occupier you'll understandably have a view on what sacrifices you're prepared to make, to accommodate everyone's needs.

Try to define where you may be willing to flex vs where you feel you might need to draw a boundary. Try to do this ahead of planning time with your partner, if you can, to give yourself an opportunity to hear your own voice. Then, when you do sit with your partner to plan all of it out, also keep an open mind and be prepared to adapt your initial views. Perhaps your partner will suggest an even better solution to one of your concerns than the one you'd already thought of?

I also wonder how you're feeling about this on an emotional level, and what you can do to help yourself here? If we take just one potential outcome here: having people come to live in your house, in *theory* gives you a stronger voice/a little more power than if it was the other way around. But, if you are a natural 'people pleaser' type, there is still a chance that in your rush to accommodate others, you very quickly de-prioritise your own needs. This may generate resentment and frustration in you, but it will also leave you with no private sanctuary to process/vent your emotions. So, you may end up giving the power you had away, and in fact placing yourself in a weaker position than you were in at the start. On the flip side, it's important to handle the power this new dynamic does afford you, and use your privilege for good, so that everyone feels secure and welcomed.

So what to do about it?

Seek the support of friends and family, as well as a trusted professional if you need a private space to talk freely and safely. The more aligned you can be with yourself, and the more embracing of the change you can be, by working with your partner to find solutions for any of the areas of concern you do feel, the better it will be for you in the long run.

If you're the parent moving in:

This may also be a tricky period of time for you. In the previous section we discussed how the parent might find themselves 'triple hatting' – as parent, as partner, and as peacekeeper, attempting to balance everyone's needs.

The same is true here, and may even feel amplified now. In the early stages of the move in particular, you may feel you need to take the lion's share of the responsibility if the children act out behaviourally, (accidentally) break things around the house, or fail to observe privacy boundaries, such as having an inquisitive look through your partner's wardrobe/drawers when they're not there etc.

In this scenario, you may feel you're relinquishing a little of the 'invisible power' you already have just by virtue of being the one with the children. The dark side of this power, of course, is that unless you're putting lots of conscious time and effort into how you're using it, it can be weaponised in a bid to get your needs met more of the time, i.e. *the reason X or Y is important is not about me at all . . . it's about the children.* This may not *always* be wholly accurate if you're being honest with yourself . . . But maybe this is something your partner has felt power*less* to challenge. So, staying with the theme of power, when you move in with your partner and your children are moving with you, you may feel as if you're suddenly giving away some of the power you had. This isn't necessarily about anyone's motivation to take it from you, rather it's a natural (and potentially unconscious) consequence of the new dynamic you're moving into.

Plus you will be mindful of the impact on the kids. It may be they're now a little further away from their schools or friends. It may be temporary, e.g. while you're both renovating a house you've bought together, or permanent, e.g. perhaps your partner's house is in a better location, or is big enough to accommodate you all. But regardless of the reasons for moving in with your partner, it may be very unsettling for the kids to be moving into a space that clearly doesn't belong to either of their parents.

As a result, the kids may feel uncomfortable, like they're treading on eggshells, or simply unsure of how life will be once you all move. This in itself, of course, is no one's fault, and is perhaps unavoidable to an extent, but there are steps you can both take to alleviate concerns and ensure everyone feels as safe and comfortable as possible.

Setting yourself up for success

First up was the triple-hat threat of parent/partner/peacekeeper. This is a normal part of parenting in a blended family, and if you can embrace this dynamic right from the early stages, this is a role you can actively play and really set the tone for a healthy family life. You can read your children better than anyone, will have an understanding of how they're feeling and be able to interpret their mood.

Equally with your partner – by knowing them really well, and equipped with the awareness that it's a huge undertaking to be part of a blended family, you'll be attuned to their needs, and sensitive when things are hard. If you can embrace this responsibility you have within your blended family and really 'step into your power' from the early stages, you will actively be creating a safe and productive environment that people can relax into.

At the same time, it's important that you don't take on too much responsibility, parents. You can apply the principle of being compassionate and sensitive here to yourself as well as to the needs of the family. Everyone in the family – including the kids – has a responsibility to themselves, to each other, and to the group. You might be in the privileged position of occupying a central position by virtue of your connections to the other members, but you are also only one person. If people act out, or behave insensitively, or have needs of their own that they're not voicing, it's important to help facilitate a dynamic where people can take responsibility, rather than trying to fix everything yourself.

Finally, in terms of the power dynamic. It's critical to keep opening up to your partner, working together to co-create the right environment where the family can flourish. You are a couple, and therefore deserve an equal voice, and equal levels of respect and care, regardless of whose house you live in.

So, try not to let a feeling that things are imbalanced get in the way of coming together as a family. As we acknowledged in the previous section, both of you may feel a little power*less* from time to time. Talking openly about these things together will no doubt help to put things into perspective, and allow you both to provide mutual reassurances.

Maybe baby

Having a baby in a blended family can be a joyful experience, perhaps especially if it is 'first time around' for one of you, or something you've been trying for for a while.

For those who already have children, or where existing children are resistant, however, the idea of having more is not always a welcome prospect, and that can be incredibly challenging for the blended couple to navigate – especially if you go on to experience loss in this area. We talk a little bit more about this sensitive subject in an upcoming chapter.

However, if you've got to the stage where you're planning or about to have a baby together, there are a few considerations to keep in mind.

A family within a family – or is it?

Having a baby will throw up all sorts of interesting conundrums for our couple – how will they relate to the child(ren) they have together, and in what way(s) may this be different from how they relate to the children they have separately, that one or both of you has been step-parenting.

If you yourself don't already have children, you cannot deny you will necessarily relate to your own baby in a different way to how you relate to your step-child(ren). Don't beat yourself up about this, as it's completely normal. Aside from the glaringly obvious fact that you will be required to actively parent this little one in a much more hands-on way than may have been necessary with your step-kids, the type of bond will of course be different.

How existing parents choose to parent this time around might well evolve too, as you move with the times and adopt contemporary child-care ideals, and enter into it with your partner. The last time you had a baby may have been some years ago, and a lot can change in that time!

All for one

However, despite the reality of your feelings and your joint parenting style, there is a clear need for both of you to be highly sensitive to the emotional needs of existing children – all of whom, including your unborn baby, are part of the same blended family you took the time to nurture together. Plus, regardless of the type of relationship, all of the children will now form a group of siblings, who will naturally compare their own status within the group to that of the others.

So, apply the same rules and same privileges to each. Unless there are significant changes to your broader circumstances that aren't specifically to do with the blended family (e.g. a different financial status), guard against applying different expectations or treatments to the kids, based on who they biologically relate to.

Plan for parenthood

Existing parents, regardless of the current best expert advice, your experience of parenthood will also be different this time around, because your teammate is different. Your unique combination of personalities and values, as well as the fact your baby will have their own unique needs, means you have an opportunity to approach things in a fresh way. That doesn't mean you have to literally start again – you cannot un-know what you already know, after all – but it does mean you shouldn't expect things to unfold in the same way. As with everything, lean in to the things you feel strongly about, and be open minded to the idea of doing things differently in other areas.

Bringing everyone together

Share the news with existing children as soon as you feel comfortable, and fold them into milestones such as scan appointments in preparation for the baby's arrival. Make them aware just how much they are loved, and reassure them there is always enough love and care to go around everyone in the family – regardless of how it grows.

Children at this stage may want to spend more time at Mum/Dad's house to be more present, and unconsciously avoid any concerns they may carry of being forgotten about. Enable this as much as you can/ are able. If the kids aren't old enough to naturally be in charge of their own arrangements, this may require working with the co-parent to come to a temporary arrangement where custody might be limited.

Once the baby has arrived, do as much as you can to bring the whole family together, allowing the kids to bond with their new baby half-brother or -sister. They could take it in turns to give their (step-) mum/(step-)dad a break, helping out with jobs like bottle feeding/ changing nappies. Then, once the baby is a little older, older kids could be invited to babysit. The more hands-on everyone can be from the start, the closer the bonds and attachments will be.

Engagement

Ooh, is an engagement on the cards? That is exciting, and generally a cause for a real celebration! One of the biggest considerations here that uniquely affects our blended family is how to tell the children involved. There are no hard and fast rights or wrongs, as your approach is going to change according to many different factors:

- The age of the children.
- Their acceptance of (and relationship with) their prospective step-parent.
- Their comfort levels with the relationship itself.
- The presence of the ex-partner (the children's other parent).

Informing your ex once you're engaged means you get to plan how to break the news – and can therefore deliver it carefully before the children have a chance to blurt it out over dinner or during the handover: 'Mummy-Mummy-guess-what-Daddy's-getting-married!' is unlikely to end your co-parent's casual Monday night on a high, even if both of you have completely moved on; it may still come as a shock to hear you are re-marrying. If the ending of your previous relationship was in the fairly recent past, doing it like this will allow a bit of space for your co-parent to process the news without the kids there, which might be needed. It acts as a courtesy to the person that you used to share your life with, and sets a respectful tone for your co-parenting relationship.

If you both have children, it will likely be slightly easier (and undoubtedly fairer) to sit them down together to let them know *when* you are engaged. That way, they can all find out at once, and there is no suggestion that one set of children have been prioritised over the other by finding out first.

If you have older kids, given how important the step-parent role is, you may decide to make them aware you're about to pop the question to their prospective step-parent. However, if your prospective fiancé(ée) also has children: beware! Telling some and not all may be really hard for your partner's kids to deal with. If they find out they weren't in the know from the start, feelings of jealousy or resentment may emerge that were entirely avoidable.

By waiting until you're engaged before they're all told together, you will:

a. be able to plan together *how* the children are told
b. ensure that no one feels left out

AND

c. be sure that all the kids have a parent around when they hear
the news, which will help them to feel safe enough to express
their feelings.

Chances are their reaction will be positive – but we want to be
eyes wide open here, and acknowledge that marriages in blended
families can be a sensitive time for the children concerned, even if
relationships are strong. They may wonder how things will change
for them, whether their mum or dad will still be as available to them
once they are *married* to someone other than their other parent. And
they may carry (irrational) feelings of disloyalty towards their other
parent: *'how can I show how happy I am for Mum and Harry, when Dad
hasn't even got a girlfriend yet and is living by himself?'* or *'I secretly really
like Carolina, and I'm looking forward to her being my step-mum – but I
think Mum is still in love with Dad and she never misses an opportunity to
insult Carolina behind the scenes.'*

So notice just how much the kids may be carrying, *in addition* to
the more positive feelings that may well be there in abundance.

You and your partner, as a newly engaged couple, will no doubt
want to bask in a glow of happiness and excitement for a while, but
if there are any difficult feelings in the house where the children are
concerned, let them share with you and express what's going on for
them. Those feelings are entirely normal, and the more you signal you
can handle a difficult conversation, and accept they might be feeling
anxious or upset, the more they'll be able to open up and begin to
process whatever it is they are experiencing. Which is the first step
towards resolving their more uncomfortable feelings, allowing them
to move towards a happier, more contented position.

If you're in the fortunate position that the children are accepting
of your relationship, and you sense that an engagement will be
treated as an exciting event, you also have the option of sharing

with them the plans for the engagement itself (maybe not quite as far as asking them to propose with you, although that's not off the table if blended family life is something you are both ultra passionate about!). But getting them involved in the planning at least could be a great way to help them buy into the prospect of gaining a step-parent, and may be a really lovely way to start to bond the family together.

With nuclear families, often the children haven't arrived by the time of the engagement, and if the children belong to the couple, there's generally less of a need to consciously reinforce the family dynamic to help everyone within it get comfortable. One of the great joys of being a part of a blended family, on the other hand, is that we can't do enough to build and then consciously reinforce the fact you're all part of the same *team*. This creates safety and a deep feeling of belonging.

If getting the kids involved in the proposal itself isn't for you, then, post-engagement, you could fold them in by having a family celebration together to mark the occasion, such as a special dinner or a party.

However you choose to do it, just remember the golden rule, which is not to underestimate the impact that even the smallest thoughtful gestures can have at this stage. The more care and consideration you/ you both put into the engagement where the children are concerned, the more they will feel part of the celebrations and new family unit right from the start.

And . . . congratulations from me!

Marriage

So now you've set the date, and are busy planning. Let's talk through some of the considerations in the lead up to the big day, as well as the event itself.

Planning

As you start to plan the wedding, the first thing to recognise is that, given you're forming a blended family, or formalising one, there is a high chance at least one of you will have been married before. Perhaps both of you. So, you'll have a chance to put your own unique stamp on the wedding that reflects you both.

It's important to give the kids a chance to adjust to the idea. This is a big event, and they will already have an awareness that marriages are a cause for celebration. On the other hand, they will also be very aware that sometimes they don't work out, based on their parents' relationship breaking down. On top of that, their other parent may not be in the position of remarriage, and so the kids might be carrying plenty of conflicting feelings.

What can you do to help?

Do give the kids time to process.

They will need to express whatever is going on for them. It's normal for them to feel a little sad or unsure. Now that you're planning the wedding, things may feel a little more real and 'serious' than when you were simply dating. Plus, the children will be able to see tangible evidence of your closeness and how important you are to each other.

If you can (both) demonstrate you understand and are open to talking about some of these more thorny topics – and not just the excitement or the lighter/breezier topics that come with planning a wedding – this approach will go a long way to ensuring the build up goes as smoothly as possible.

Don't hide things!

If you feel the kids are, in part, struggling to adjust to the idea they will soon have an official 'step-parent', or that Mum or Dad is moving on and making a serious commitment, try to resist the temptation to minimise the planning process. Examples of this may include hiding supplier brochures that you picked up at last week's wedding fayre, or avoiding talking about the elements of the planning process you're engrossed in.

While it may seem appealing in the moment to avoid upset or a difficult conversation, minimising won't ultimately help to resolve any difficult feelings that are lurking in the background for any member of the family, and it may actually have the opposite effect – to hinder. Why? Well, getting married is a Big Deal – and requires a lot of planning and effort to organise properly. So if you are actively hiding or minimising things when the kids are around, there's a high chance one (or both) member(s) of the couple will start to feel resentful, which could cause a problem for the relationship. Burying your engaged head in the sand also won't help the child(ren) move towards a healthier place of acceptance and happiness.

Instead, use the planning process as an opportunity to generate some excitement among the kids. There are three ways you can do this:

1. Ask how they would like to be involved.
2. Seek their views about elements of the planning, but only those things you're happy for them to have a view on. Some things are for the couple to decide, especially if this is the first time

around for at least one of you. Smaller things, however, such as hairstyles or choosing from a shortlisted choice of bands for the evening entertainment, may be a great way to help spark their interest and enthusiasm.

3. Give them space to open up, rather than shy away from a difficult conversation.

Roles

A great way to help the children look forward to the wedding itself is to allocate them roles.

Some ideas for younger children:

- Flower girl
- Page boy
- Sharing a reading together or with an adult

Some ideas for older/adult children:

- Doing a reading solo
- Giving the bride away
- Best man
- Bridesmaid

Or perhaps there's another role even more suited to your kids? Of course, you don't need me to tell you that a wedding is not needed to create the blended family. Marriage is not for everyone, and you may choose to simply cohabit instead. But, if marriage *is* important for you as a blended couple, then the marriage itself becomes not just a wedding between the two of you, it signals the 'official' cementing of the blended family itself. So, the more you can fold the children in to be a part of the event, the more you will be signalling to them just how seriously you care for them and see them as an intrinsic part of the new family.

> When my mum married my step-father, I was asked to be the best man. I thought it was a really nice gesture; he could have asked any number of friends, yet he chose me. I guess that showed how much family life meant to him. As the years have gone on, we've become closer and closer, to the point where I now consider him to be a close friend as well as a parent. I'm now in my own step-family, and when we get married, I'd love for my kids to have a role in our wedding. For me, to not actively include them is the same thing as excluding them – which wouldn't set the right tone at all.
>
> *George, father and step-son (42)*

There are no hard and fast rules regarding whether you should invite your co-parent to the wedding. You will know what's best for your family and the people involved. At this stage, you may all be socialising together and perhaps that feels fine. But perhaps you never socialise at all and the idea of your ex (or your partner's ex) attending your wedding is making you anxious? If so, remember these two things:

1. Only invite your ex if it's something *both* you and your fiancé(e) want. This isn't something to do just because your kids think Mummy or Daddy would be upset if they weren't invited. It can cause lots of stress, and make all of you in the dynamic (you, your fiancé (s), your kids, your ex, your family members, your

friends) feel awkward. Plus, unless you all feel so comfortable around each other already that you feel it would be odd *not to* invite them, you may spend time worrying about how to handle things on the day, and now is not the time to give yourself unnecessary stress.

2. Even if both of you are relaxed about it, only invite your ex if you are sure that in the event they accept, they're happy to do so (as opposed to attending because the children really want them there). Someone feeling obliged to attend, so they don't appear to be churlish or rude by turning an invitation down, will have to put a brave face on things when inside they may feel sad, self-conscious or awkward. While 'disaster' may feel a bit too strong a word here – it's certainly a recipe for upset, which can easily be avoided.

Speeches

When planning content for the speeches, it's easy to reflect on how happy you are now, in your *new* dynamic. Or, to wax lyrical about the differences between the old you, 'shackled' by your old marriage, and the new you since you've found love with X, and how proud you are of how much you've changed/grown. Yes, you may well think these things, and you would be forgiven for wanting to let the world know!

But . . . and for the love of all things blended, please please guard against allowing any of these sentiments to filter into the speeches (and this goes for any of them, not just your own). Instead, keep the content focused on the happy couple and the blended family, and avoid any sort of past/present comparisons. This approach demonstrates good boundaries, as well as courtesy and respect for your current and ex-partners. You will also be saving the children from having to contend with a whole host of tricky feelings, especially on a day where emotions will already be heightened.

Finally, we'll end this section with the introduction of the Family Moon . . .

Whether it's a few days glamping or a few weeks in some exotic hideaway, like most newly married couples, you'll likely be looking forward to a honeymoon to celebrate the wedding and the start of married life together. This is important and definitely a great opportunity to invest in your relationship.

But, the blended family can also uniquely use this as an opportunity to recognise the start of their life together, as a team. Enter: The Family Moon. The Family Moon is an extra option you have available to you, in addition to the couples honeymoon you might take. If you both have kids, it's a lovely way to consciously bring them all into the equation and recognise that taking this step also means the official start to the blended family you're all a part of. You can use the Family Moon concept as a lovely way to get everyone involved, discussing locations that would work for you all, or planning special activities you can do while away etc.

I want to make it clear here that the sentiment of the Family Moon is *not* reliant on spending money you may not have – this has to be something that's completely accessible to you, regardless of your financial situation. Just like any holiday, you're simply going to be tailoring your unique Family Moon according to your budget. You could, plan the Family Moon in for the year after you get married, say, or to coincide with another trip you typically make as a family – for example, if you normally go away during the holiday season. Or maybe your Family Moon looks like a staycation vs a trip abroad. Whatever your circumstances, you can apply the *concept* of a noteworthy holiday to uniquely mark your new family unit. Blended families I work with tell me how important this was for them, and how much it meant to everyone involved.

During this chapter we've spent time covering a few of the milestones that our blended couples will face during their life together. Each will bring their own unique highs and lows. Some will feel surprisingly easy, and no doubt you'll have your own top tips and anecdotes to pass on to others to help them with their own journey. Other milestones, however (and usually the ones you expected would be a walk in the park!), may feel like you're fighting an uphill battle, catching you off guard and landing a blow when you least expect. In your own blended family, you will undoubtedly experience other firsts as part of your journey together that we haven't been able to touch upon here. However, ultimately, if you both can remember to approach each one with a conscious and positive mindset, you won't go far wrong.

6

Handling Conflict

Conflict handling and resolution is a really big subject, and it's certainly a hot topic for our blended families. Before we talk more about this, and the options you have for dealing with it, let's go back to basics to help us understand why we tend to struggle with it.

For many, conflict is directly associated with arguments, tension and stress. In my private practice, I witness time and again how people run from the idea of dealing with difficult situations consciously – whether that's calling out unhelpful behaviours, offering constructive feedback, or simply expressing their own needs – for fear of some sort of negative reprisal. And while there is often a difference in exactly how people respond to conflict in the workplace vs in private, at home, their underlying relationship with it remains the same.

The connection between authority and conflict

We know that our *relationship* with conflict is not just related to conflict itself, and what it means to us as individuals. It's also related to our relationship with authority. To make this point, we can take a quick trip back to childhood. This formative period of our lives is the bedrock of our learning when it comes to our relationship with conflict. Whether or not we believe it is acceptable to express ourselves authentically in the world . . . how we feel about approaching what we perceive to be potential conflict . . . how we respond when it arises around us.

It is also during our childhood that we witness the example our primary caregivers (and therefore authority figures) set us, through observing their behaviour towards each other, and how we were treated by them. During childhood too, we learned to distinguish between how conflict feels with three different groups, depending on the power balance within each type of relationship:

1. Those who have authority over us.
2. Those who have equal power to us.
3. Those we have authority over.

Those who have more authority than us

Perhaps we had a difficult experience with authority figures, e.g. grandparents, parents or step-parents, or schoolteachers? Perhaps they abused their power, e.g. through coercive, critical or shaming behaviours? These behaviours can easily limit our capacity to value and be kind to ourselves, and the extent to which we feel we can advocate for ourselves and share our opinions.

Alternatively, perhaps we had strong boundaries modelled to us, and learned it was okay to make mistakes; those in authority used their power wisely – to guide, inspire, teach.

Those who have equal power to us

Conflict between peers may seem easier for some, as no one is obviously 'in charge'. In a family, our peer relationships include our siblings, and specifically in a blended family this will extend to half-siblings or step-siblings. We are on an equal footing with our peers, which can therefore make it easier for some to speak more freely and approach difficult conversations, as the stakes are perceived to be lower.

On the other hand, it is precisely this freedom that can make conflict between peers particularly challenging for others. Because peers aren't in a position of authority, they can be less likely to watch and manage their words and behaviours when communicating. This can leave the person on the receiving end of the conflict open to attack and consequently they may move into a defensive position quickly to deal with the situation. Because we aren't in a position of authority relative to our peers, we don't have the luxury of feeling inherently safer in the dynamic.

Those we have authority over

Finally, in childhood we also started to learn how we preferred to behave when we ourselves were in authority. For example, how we treated younger siblings, half-siblings or step-siblings, or even pets in the family household. As you can imagine, how we learned to treat those we had power over will in turn be influenced by how *we* were treated. If we were abused in some way – belittled, excluded, made fun of etc – we may unconsciously take the impact of that treatment out on others, or replicate the behaviours. You may have heard of the saying 'the abused become the abuser', which is a neat way of summarising the point.

Or, if we are conscious of it, we may deliberately choose to use our negative experiences for good, and actively take a different approach, so as not to hand down the same woundings to the next generation.

Step aside for five

Exercise: Exploring conflict and authority

Take a moment in a quiet space, close your eyes, and reflect on the following questions:

- What does authority mean to me?
- What does conflict mean to me?
- What was my experience of both of these things when I was a child?
- What was my experience of both of these things when I was a teenager/young adult?
- What is my experience of both of these things now that I am an adult?
- How has my relationship with conflict and authority changed over time?

Firstly, note down your feelings as you consider each of these questions. How did the exercise make you feel? Were there any questions that you felt a stronger reaction to than others?

Now note down your thoughts. Perhaps you can remember certain words that are important, or perhaps the questions jogged your memory and you have recalled scenes or experiences that impacted (for good or bad) in some way.

Next, have a think about your answers, and what impact your relationship with conflict and authority is having in your blended family. Consider:

- Are there any members of the family that I experience conflict with in particular? What is my insight into that, based on what I now know of myself?
- Are there any members of the family I avoid having any sort of conflict with?
- Are there times when I feel like I've said too much, or behaved in an unhelpful way? What do I notice about those times?
- Are there times when I feel I've not said enough? What do I notice about those times?

I wonder what conclusions you can draw from your answers to these questions? Treat them all as information. At this stage it's also important to cut yourself a little slack, as turning the spotlight on yourself in this way can feel tiring and intense. But it's the first step to getting conscious – and getting conscious means:

- Learning to recognise what (if anything) might be holding you back in your blended family.
- Shedding light on how you could be hindering the family dynamic.
- Showing yourself your areas of strength.
- Highlighting your positive contributions to the household.

Conflict occurs for lots of reasons; some general themes include:

- A difference in opinion, perspective or values.
- A desire to protect or defend self.
- A desire to protect or defend others.
- A feeling that our boundaries are being walked all over.

Let's say a little more about each one so we're all on the same page.

Conflict arising from difference (opinions, perspectives or values)

Received wisdom tells us that in our external environments we will encounter many people whose views oppose ours, for a host of reasons. However, understanding and tolerating differences in our respective lived experiences is the tip of the iceberg for our blended families. Here, we need to consider different personality styles too, if they're compatible, and to what extent how we choose to express ourselves is conducive to our blended family dynamic.

Where some are naturally more direct and forthright than others, some prefer to be a little quieter and go with the flow. The convergence of multiple 'strong' personalities on a domestic front can often make for a very vocal and direct household dynamic.

Where this more direct sort of style meets a more gentle, delicate character, it can create balance in the household – some members will be louder and take up more space, whereas some are naturally quieter; there's a place for everyone.

In others, however, it can feel jarring, and a long period of adjustment may be necessary, to help foster understanding and find areas of commonality. But any additional conflict in this family dynamic can also be a real blessing in disguise. Family members are more likely to know where they stand, and grievances are more likely to be aired.

It stands to reason that conflict will inevitably arise in our blended families, given we regularly encounter those who see the world differently to us. Moreover, our blended families will be full of conflicting personality styles, who haven't yet had the chance to establish a shared understanding and tolerance of the differences that *are* present, by virtue of living together in close proximity for years. And, by not being *directly* related to our step-relations, there is a lower chance values will be similar/compatible to the others living in the household – at least at first, until the blended family has established and characters have had time to harmonise, or even synchronise. It is partly for this reason that some commentators in this field reject the idea of the blended family altogether – for them the concept is far too idealistic and far from their reality.

Yet, it's only as we encounter difference that we have an opportunity to learn and ultimately grow, and for our families to flourish. This is nothing new, as we see this principle everywhere. In medicine, we are taught that a diverse gut microbiome keeps us in optimal health. We see it in nature – the natural world will always adapt and introduce diversity in its drive to survive. We see it in the workplace, where we know we need a range of different perspectives and mindsets sitting around an executive table to achieve the best results. Where humans encounter difference, often we encounter conflict, as we have been taught to fear the potential threat – we sense on a very deep level that difference means danger. So it is precisely *because* conflict can signal difference that we know it serves a useful purpose here in our blended families – to raise up the consciousness and standards of the whole system, and help it to thrive.

We've seen that the levels of conflict our blended family will encounter will depend on the type and strength of innate differences felt by its members. But it also depends on the *number* of people that are a part of the blended family. To illustrate the point, let's look at arguably one of the more complex blended family types – those where both members of the couple bring children together.

Where both members of the couple bring children together, it can make the likelihood of conflict a little higher than in other types of blended family – for example, those where only one member of the couple has had children. Why?

Well, we're talking more personalities to balance, more views of varying strength that may or may not align, and of course we can't forget loyalty. Where we have blended families, we generally have divided loyalties. And where we have two parents with two sets of children, not only do we want to protect the children we already have, but we're balancing the existing role of parent with the *new* role of step-parent we're learning to get the hang of, as well as our desire to protect our partner.

To add further complexity, step-siblings are more likely to want to support their own parent when there are differences (either passively or explicitly), which may cause tension between the step-siblings, depending on the strength of their relationship. Especially if they are young enough to all be living in the same house and haven't yet flown the nest. So as you can see, power dynamics may be particularly tricky in this type of household, particularly in the early stages, as everyone adjusts to their multiple roles, their new relationships, and finally their position within the group.

At the other end of the scale, you might think that where only one member of the couple brings only one child to the new family there will consequently be more harmony, based on the simple fact there are less people and therefore less personalities to get to know and balance over time. Sadly this is not always the case. As a classic triangular dynamic is formed, step-parents can often feel highly excluded, and often feel scapegoated if any disagreement or conflict arises. Parents can be perceived to 'side' with their child(ren) regardless of the situation, and the step-child can look to blame the step-parent, as the relative 'newcomer' to the dynamic. When the step-parent raises this with their partner, the partner can feel tremendous pressure – perhaps feeling a need to choose between defending their child or advocating for their partner, or mediating between the two, which can be exhausting. Or, of course, the adult couple can come together as a united team, very much at the detriment of the emotional needs of the child.

So it can all feel like a bit of a minefield at this stage, and you'd be forgiven for feeling overwhelmed and a little bit hopeless. Don't worry, though. Later on we shall be looking at some of the practical things you can all do to alleviate difficulties that may arise, and equip you with some tools to help manage conflict in a healthier way.

Conflict arising from a desire to protect yourself

When we feel attacked we can, in an instant, move from feeling calm and relaxed to feeling as though we're under threat. And our bodily and physiological responses are so automatic and instinctive that quite often we aren't able to wait to sense the difference between what poses a real genuine threat and what is an unconscious overreaction of our nervous system.

Our nervous systems can mobilise when a literal physical attack or danger isn't present at all – here we can consider much more subtle experiences of being threatened, such as being snapped at, taken to task, or shamed in a public group environment. For our blended families, this might be something as simple as an admonishment over the dinner table, or being on the receiving end of some pointed sarcasm, courtesy of your step-children. So, we respond to the threat in the best ways our instincts know how – we freeze (finding ourselves unable to speak or respond), we take flight (disengaging from the conversation or wanting desperately to leave the room), or we fight (verbally, if not physically).

Conflict arising where we feel protective of others

In the wild, the animal kingdom will often stop at nothing to defend their young – picture the lioness defending her cubs, for example. The same can be said for parents who feel the need to protect their children. This is particularly heightened in the blended family, where the children are being routinely looked after or socialised with at least one adult who isn't their parent. Here, as in any classical fairy story, the scene is set for someone in the house to unconsciously play or be put into the role of persecutor (wicked witch), someone in the dynamic to feel attacked, who becomes our victim (damsel in distress), and, finally, for someone to feel the need to rescue or defend the victim (Prince Charming).

Crucially, though, we humans have a unique ability to tailor the position we take in response to what we see, based on our own *conscious* interpretation of it. And, in turn, our own unique interpretation will be based on our own learned experiences, our own values and our relationship with the other family members.

These factors can change according to our perception of how other family members are treated. So, each one of our blended family members can move into any of these roles at any time. We are not, and cannot be, limited by the traditional instincts of a parent protecting their child, based on the complex family systems we have developed in the blended family world. Consider the following examples:

#1 Karen is angry with her step-father, for becoming exasperated with her mum, for not having done X or Y – which has upset Karen's mum. Karen cannot believe her step-father would talk to her mum in such a way, and is planning to make sure he knows exactly how she feels.

#2 Steve is furious, as his step-son Mark has just disrespected him one too many times. He feels powerless to do anything – so Mark's mum steps in to defend Steve by reprimanding Mark.

#3 Natalia feels the need to protect her step-daughter, Daniella, after her wife Nadia (Daniella's mum) has hit a raw nerve when she teased her over dinner. She loves her wife and knows she might not have meant it, but she can be pretty insensitive and doesn't always notice the impact she has.

And each of these roles can shift based on the response of the other two characters in the dynamic. To demonstrate the point, let's take another look at scenario #2, from the point at which we left off:

Mark has just been told off by his mum . . . he now feels so embarrassed that he has been shouted at in front of the family that he goes red and quiet and withdraws from the family conversation. Steve, who a moment ago was furious with Mark, now feels sorry for him. He knows what it's like to feel shamed in front of a group – unbeknownst to Mark it was in fact the story of Steve's own childhood. So, he asks his wife to back off as he's sure Mark didn't mean to hurt him . . .

Notice how the roles have completely changed, with each person's position rotating as they respond to how comfortable they feel within each role, or observing someone else respond to the one they're in? So now Mark's mum takes the position of victim – shamed as she now feels by her husband – which is ironic given it was him she was trying to defend!

You can imagine yourself in a similar position perhaps, and when you reflect on your own experiences here, you can perhaps empathise with all three characters – Mark, Steve, and Mark's mum. If you have been in this situation too, you'll recall just how quickly things can escalate beyond anything anyone could have consciously prepared for. In a matter of seconds, it can feel as if everyone has become defensive, preparing to leave the room, taking sides, raising voices etc.

It is this speed that reveals the bear trap when trying to deal with conflict within a blended family. In a professional context, at work, people generally try to contain or manage the strength of their personal responses, for fear of behaving inappropriately, being judged negatively by colleagues, or being taken to task by HR. But in a blended family, where emotions run high, resolutions can sometimes take a bit more time as bonds often aren't as deep vs those in a nuclear family. Dealing with conflict only in an automatic way – through instinctive responses – can create problems for the household.

Conflict arising through a feeling of being walked all over

Being walked all over is another way of saying our boundaries are being ignored, and this can show up in our blended families in a number of ways. Here are a few examples:

- People walking into rooms without knocking. Particularly common for little children who, for example, are used to walking into Mum or Dad's room, and now have to be mindful that their step-mum/step-dad shares the space and needs privacy. Or, adults walking into teenager's rooms, or unlocked bathrooms without thinking. Teenagers are famously protective of their personal space, but this sense of territory is understandably heightened when an adult who isn't their parent makes this mistake.

- Step-children feeling their step-parent is taking more of a parental role than is wanted or needed.
- Step-parents feeling adult step-children are being overly interfering/judgemental in their romantic relationship with their parent.
- Parents working too hard to integrate their partners and children together before the dynamic is ready for it, i.e. 'Kids . . . Mother's Day is coming up, aren't you going to send Ellie some flowers?'

Want to develop a healthier relationship with conflict? Try these three things:

Get conscious

Have a think back to when you did the exercise earlier on in the chapter. It might have seemed intense . . . like there was lots to look at, and you might have been left wondering: where on earth am I going to start?! But what I'd like you to hold on to is that all of this takes time just to notice there's something going on in the first place – but even *more* time to unpick.

Cognitive awareness and understanding is only the *first* part of the work here. If you are someone who would describe themselves as having a negative relationship with authority, or who is conflict averse, then building the *new* neural pathways that are needed to change your relationship with authority and learn to *embrace* conflict isn't going to happen overnight.

But you can do it, step-by-step. Start off by noticing when you feel yourself responding negatively to conflict. Have a think after the event about how you could have handled things a bit differently. Here is a great opportunity to be curious about what was going on for you in the moment, and you can use some of the questions I asked you in the exercise earlier in the chapter to get started. By conducting your own mini review – like a post-match analysis – you will start to spot patterns that were invisible to you before, when you weren't really thinking consciously about how you typically respond in moments of conflict.

Be really kind to yourself during this process. The patterns you may uncover might show you that you can often use really hurtful words when you feel attacked, for example. Or that you fear conflict with one person in the household in particular. Or that your style means you find it hard to stay in the room when conflict is present – you like to take flight rather than stay and have what you expect will be an uncomfortable conversation. The possibilities are endless.

Your responses are simply how you cope when you're feeling stressed, to try and protect yourself. So remember: you're not perfect, you're a human being. When you're working through things in this way, it's helpful to simply notice what's going on, suspending judgement. And now you're working hard to spot what might be very unhelpful behavioural patterns, you're one step closer to being able to address them – and that's a really good thing!

Unlock your own growth mindset

In order to learn to embrace the opportunities that conflict can bring, you're going to need plenty of patience, a commitment to continued self-awareness, and what we call a growth mindset.

A growth mindset is described by many different practitioners, but the jist of what it means is:

- Being open to change.
- Thinking flexibly, allowing perspectives to shift and alter as you receive new information, and with the passage of time.
- Using your imagination to envision what you'd like to happen in your life, and not limiting your ability to achieve the goals you set for yourself.
- Digging deep to find the humility required to step forward and take responsibility, when you inevitably do show up in ways that aren't helpful.

Developing a growth mindset is one of the most important things you can do for yourself. It's what will help you to get conscious, take responsibility for your life, define your goals and manifest the kind of life you would love to have. Where conflict is concerned, a growth mindset is particularly helpful as it stops us from feeling afraid of it, and allows us to be curious: *How can I see this as an opportunity to grow? What do I need to learn from this person? Can I try something different to develop the sorts of relationships I'd love to have?*

You will know you're adopting a growth mindset as your perspective will shift from:

- Conflict is scary and I'm anxious about it.
- I shy away from hearing the things that frustrate you about me.
- I find it hard to talk to you about the things that I find frustrating in our relationship.

To

- Conflict is a normal experience – it's an inevitable part of our life that can enhance my relationships, if I allow it rather than fear it.

- I look forward to talking through our differences; if I don't know how you feel, how can I grow?
- I seek to share my own views and feelings, and I want to actively listen to and hear yours, to improve my relationship with you, and make our family life even better.

Be brave

When you start noticing your behavioural patterns, you will start to develop a deeper appreciation of the things that really bother you when conflict arises in your blended family, and things that you might need to try to alleviate any tension.

In the following exercise, which I've devised based on principles we might use in couples therapy, you're invited to think about some things you can try in the moment to make things a bit easier for you. Grab a pen and paper, and tackle these three sentences, which relate to how conflict is handled within the couple dynamic. Ideally, do this exercise alongside your partner. There's no point in flying solo here, as the dynamic between you both is down to the uniqueness you each bring. So, when tackling conflict, while it's important to really think about how you show up personally, often the quickest way to resolve conflict is to work on the underlying *relational dynamic* with the other person.

1. When I experience conflict with my partner, the things I tend to do that are unhelpful include . . .
2. Some things I could do to help the situation include . . .
3. Some things I would like to ask my partner to do to help the situation include . . .

Now that you've made your own unique list, share them with one another and talk them through together.

Resolving conflict with young people

Where young children are concerned, the task is more about how you set boundaries vs deal with conflict management, as you both do the job of parenting or looking after the kids. But as the kids become teens or young adults, in developing their own views about what's right and wrong, they will begin the natural process of separating out from their parents and authority figures. So, here, it's entirely appropriate to raise the subject with them – especially if you are concerned that your relationship seems to be characterised by excessive conflict.

It's worth pointing out that most minor disagreements are resolved quickly and don't necessarily need to be 'managed'. But if you're finding there is excessive conflict in the household, you will find a more conscious approach will help to nip it in the bud sooner.

Resolving bigger conflicts with younger people

Firstly, you're going to want to think about the environment – this is key to laying the foundations for a productive outcome. Having the conversation when you're both relatively calm means choosing a moment when you both have a bit of time, are feeling relaxed, and are in a place where you can hear each other – without other family members getting in the way.

Remember you are the adult and the authority figure in the dynamic, whether you like it or not. Clearly, however, this doesn't mean you get to talk how you like or adopt a 'what I say goes' attitude!

Instead, being the authority figure means you have extra responsibility to consider how and when the conversation happens, ensuring it stands the best possible chance of running smoothly. It means you can role model attitudes such as a willingness to listen, and respect. When giving some thought as to how you might want to approach a conversation with them proactively, do make allowances for their age, and their relationship with you, ensuring the content and tone of the conversation is age appropriate.

Two possible approaches include:

1. For generalised challenges, e.g. a difficult relationship borne out of jealousy:
   a. Open up the conversation by firstly talking about the relationship you'd ideally like to have together, and why it matters to you.
   b. Name what seems to be getting in the way, and how it is making you feel.
   c. Then, check-in with the other person and ask them to reflect back to you what they heard.
   d. Invite them to share their own views on A and B, and then reflect back to them what you heard.
   Use the rest of the conversation to gradually work through what you've both shared, clearly and respectfully, in order to reach some sort of a resolution.

This way of resolving conflict doesn't go into too much depth, as would be appropriate with your partner, who is an adult and your relational 'equal'. The broad subject matter may feel less scarier, safer and more conceptual to a younger person than a much more specific topic. By starting on a positive note, you're also signalling to your young person that you're aiming to have a great relationship with them – and that there's lots of opportunity to work on it together.

Take things gently, without trying to force the conversation or a resolution, especially if the other person is reluctant. Sometimes, just knowing that someone cares enough to try to work on the relationship is enough to help the other soften just a little. And if you can let the other person know they matter to you, and you're here to talk when they're ready, that in itself is a positive signal that will gradually build trust while you're waiting for them to step forward and lean into things.

The approach of talking generally about the relationship is a sort of 'slow and steady' way forward, and it may take a little time before you get back on track. Try to be patient; these things pay off with a little perseverance.

Or . . .

2. For particular subjects that seem to crop up time and again, you might choose to talk about these scenarios specifically:
    a. Try to define what it is that needs resolving. This step often gets missed out – people take for granted that the reason for the upset is obvious to both parties. However, you'd be amazed at how often, when asked exactly the same question, two people relating to one another can have totally different views as to what's causing the issues. What one finds upsetting, the other might be oblivious to – it may be something completely different that's been winding them up. So it's worth asking the question, ensuring both of you are on the same page from the start. (NB: Where you have different ideas of what's causing harm to the relationship, make a note of all of them so you can talk about them one-by-one.)
    b. Find out, why is it a problem *now*? It might be that the

current situation wasn't always a problem, but one person's feelings have changed towards it for some reason that isn't clear to the other. Talk about what's changed, and how that change has impacted you (both).

c. What do you think is contributing to the problem? Is there one big thing or a series of smaller changes or events that are causing difficulties?

d. Finally, what do both of you think might help you work towards a resolution? Where there are multiple ideas, try and settle on the top one or two things that seem the most achievable for you both. Trying to create lots of new habits all at once is much harder than simply focusing on one or two things.

In our blended family, my mum and step-dad's parenting styles were really different to my dad and step-mum's. I know each household works differently, but from a child's perspective it was really confusing. When I look back I can see that the only one who seemed to have no difficulty in setting behavioural expectations was my step-mum. She wasn't mean particularly, just what you might call firm. She probably felt frustrated, and felt she was the only one trying to do any parenting at times. I could also see that every time she tried to set a boundary, it caused a lot of friction between her and Dad, who didn't often tell us off – he wanted to create a dynamic where he was our friend. But that made my siblings and I blame her a lot for any difficulties we felt. I think that's my top tip for other blended families out there – don't leave it to just one person to set the expectations. Plus, once they're defined, try and be consistent with what's expected, and then everyone can follow suit.

Andrew, adult step-child (46)

The luxury of reading a chapter in a book like this that's dedicated to conflict is that we're talking *idealistically* about conflict resolution. It can't take into account the *realistic* facts, which are that lives are incredibly busy, we have emotional swings, and we're not always mutually willing to resolve things in the first place. In real life, resolving our differences takes time, as we're not perfect, and we're trying to juggle a million different things all at once. So, to finish up, try and hold on to these four points:

1. Conflict is going to happen. Aagghhh – but also . . . ahhhh, breathe. The sooner you work with it and try to focus on getting your (major) differences resolved, the sooner you can move to a more harmonious state of equilibrium, and focus on the joy of connection, growth, fun and building memories.
2. When you're feeling uncomfortable, especially at home in your private space, time can seem to pass incredibly slowly. But remember that all emotional states are transient; things will pass and get better.
3. As one of the authority figures in the blended family, you can play a big role in resolving any conflict, by dealing proactively with tough situations.
4. You and your partner are a team, and should work together on the approach that's right for your household. Lean on each other – go for dinner, have a cuppa, take a walk, talk and make time for each other. Then, finally, once you've agreed how to handle a situation – stick to what you've agreed.

7

The Blended Family
in its Early Stages

Coming together is an exciting time for our blended families. By now a bit of time has passed, everyone has met one another, you may have even moved in together – and you're starting to settle into the new normal of domestic life.

So now's a great time to pause for a moment and appraise the health of your new family. We'll take a moment in this chapter to have a think about how you can find the right balance for you, between voicing and getting your own needs met, as well as encouraging an environment where other family members feel equally comfortable voicing *their* needs, and working with each other to find a way to get them met that works for everyone. Then we'll get a bit more specific, and appreciate some of the unique characteristics that define inter-blended family relationships. But first, we're going to think about some general points that will get you on your way to setting up a really healthy and safe dynamic.

Things don't need to be the way they used to be

Number one on this list is the first principle of: 'Always keep in mind this is a new blended family unit.' This means you all get to define the rules and ways of being that keep everyone happy (most of the time, at least), and that takes into consideration how everyone's feeling, and what each person needs.

'Hovis' best of both

Back in the early 2000s, when Hovis developed this ground-breaking loaf, it seemed the answers to people's yeast-related prayers. White bread lovers were promised all the taste of the loaf they loved, while those looking for a more rounded hit of nutritional goodness were also satisfied. And what on earth does all of this have to do with blended families? Well, quite a lot actually. This is about embracing your lifestyle. Let's say you have custody of the children half of the time. Well, how lovely that you get to combine a hands-on parenting role with spending quality time with your partner to connect, to socialise, or to double down on your professional life. Remember the growth mindset we talked about in Chapter Six? This is about positively reframing your circumstances, to ensure you can see the best of both domestic worlds that you are a part of.

But this opportunity to acknowledge the best of both doesn't start and stop with your lifestyle. In the times where the blended family are all together, you're going to come up against any number of micro situations where people have different views or preferences. Whereas in Chapter Six we looked at where difference results in conflict, these types of micro-differences simply signal a more peaceful opportunity for listening and for compromise.

An example of this is watching TV. A blended couple I spoke to recently, Hugh and Carrie, described how Hugh's teenage daughter, living in the household, had become used to dictating what the family watched on TV in the main living area. In order to help her adjust to the dynamic, the blended couple (driven by Dad) had allowed this to continue over a number of months.

Hugh had indulged his only child here in order to soothe his own conflict-avoidant style, and minimise the guilty feelings he was carrying. But, it soon became apparent that this was *not* a case of 'least said soonest mended'. In fact, the lack of conscious consideration for everyone in the household had started to cause resentment in Carrie, which in turn was causing unspoken challenges in the relationship she had with her seventeen-year-old step-daughter. It was also fuelling conflict in the couple relationship.

This is a dynamic that can all too easily arise in our blended family, as a direct result of guilt and over-compensating. In this case you could argue that one person's needs were being completely ignored in favour of another family member.

I wonder how you would handle this situation in your blended family?

Getting your own needs met

This topic is a big one– and is certainly not limited to the subject of blended families. It shows up in individuals who lack time/space for themselves personally, and in relationships too, where it can present significant challenges for couples.

We are all human with a series of needs ranging from survival (e.g. eating) to basic (e.g. eating a balanced diet) to discretionary (e.g. indulging in our favourite foods), but so many people believe that articulating any form of need other than the most basic is selfish, or an indulgence that shouldn't be tolerated. What a shame! Because creating boundaries around what we realistically do and do not have capacity to do keeps us healthy. Gabor Mate, the Candian physician, describes this wonderfully and in detail in his book *When the Body Says No: The Cost of Hidden Stress* (2003), which highlights the direct connection between the mind and the body, and demonstrates how stress can harm us. If we forget how to tune into what we need, we then stand no chance of being able to articulate those needs clearly to those around us. To top it all off, we can, in turn, judge others who are able to do this, by calling them selfish, indulgent or inconsiderate.

If this pattern persists, it can create resentment between the couple. One half is great at getting their needs met – for example, by speaking up when things become too much, slowing down when overwhelmed, or readily volunteering to take care of tasks they are good at or have lots of capacity to do. The other, however, who is less good at articulating and meeting their needs, might martyr themselves at the altar of household chores, thinking to themselves: *'I'm exhausted, but if I don't do it all, no one else will.'* As a result, they feel cross with their partner for not pulling their weight around the house (according to their perception). Meanwhile, their partner simply can't understand why the other doesn't seem to be able to voice when they are struggling, and becomes frustrated with their martyrdom (according to their perception).

This topic is important to address, because the degree to which the couple are skilled at identifying and meeting their own needs will impact the overall smooth running of our blended families. If you buy into the fact that getting your own needs met is important, you're more likely to encourage others to do the same, and to celebrate when people have the courage to voice what it is *they* need. And the more conscious the communication, the happier and safer the dynamic will be.

Recognising the importance of identifying your needs and working to get them met is another way of saying you take responsibility for yourself, for solving your own needs or reaching out to family members if you need support from others. By doing this you make it safe for others to lean on the family if they have a greater need they can't meet alone, and by meeting your own needs you're creating space for others to get their needs met. Through this process you will also demonstrate just how much you value yourself, which unconsciously cues others to treat you similarly – with respect and kindness – and, moreover, you'll be role modelling healthy behaviour to other members of the family.

Spotting the needs of others

Hopefully by now you've got the jist, that ensuring your own needs are met is incredibly important. But how do you ensure you're doing all you can to look after the needs of others? We need to clarify here – helping to look after the needs of others does not mean doing everything for them. It means doing what you can to ensure the family you're creating is aware that it will function optimally, if each individual component (i.e. each member of the household) is as motivated and satisfied as possible.

In this way, it's not unlike leading or managing a team in the workplace. Yes, the goals of the whole team are important, but how can it perform at its best unless each individual is also happy and energised enough to contribute to the bigger picture?

So, your role here extends to not just helping to identify and manage your own needs, but empowering each family member to have their own voice, equipping them with the confidence to raise things that might be on their mind, or to suggest changes (however small) or family habits to adopt that might make a big difference to them personally. Common topics might include not forgetting to put the toilet seat down, or not leaving tea bags in the sink.

There are going to be certain members you and the rest of the family will naturally be more aware of supporting, who are dependent on the input of others – babies, young children or those who are less able, for example. And, of course, some will be more inclined to say when something is wrong, or share what would make them happy – the naturally more confident or extroverted individuals perhaps. But what about those who are naturally quieter, or who may lack the self-esteem to realise how important their needs are? Or, those who are simply struggling with life (difficulties at work, elderly parents to look after etc) and who may not have taken the time to sit and think about what might help to alleviate their stress?

As the family starts to integrate, now is a great time to think about how you can instil a mindset where each member not only places value on their own health and needs – in all senses of the word, emotional, physical, physiological and psychological – but also that of the others.

Brené Brown, American researcher and professor, perhaps best known for her work on shame and vulnerability, describes this as conducting a 'family gap analysis', which is a simple exercise designed to identify what needs to get done and who has the capacity to fill the gap during tricky moments or particular junctions of stress. You, however, can apply this tactic as an everyday mindset. And here we're not (necessarily) talking about bigger asks, such as getting a dog, someone wanting their room decorating, or changing routines such as the division of household tasks.

We're talking about much smaller day-to-day things, like keeping the house a little quieter during exam periods, noticing when someone seems a little preoccupied and checking in on them, making a cup of tea for someone who's had a tough day, prioritising someone's desire to watch that new show everyone is talking about after revising hard all day. Or, in the example we used a little earlier on in the chapter, it's Hugh remembering Carrie's need to unwind and feel like she belongs in the household is just as important as the need his daughter has to feel like *she's* an important and much wanted member of the family unit – and consequently proactively helping to balance the needs of both without causing unnecessary tension.

Inter-family relationships

In the embryonic stages of the family's development, unique inter-family relationships begin to form. There is no one-size-fits-all approach; each relationship is going to be affected by the broader circumstances. But we will talk in general terms about some of the things to consider and the many strengths of these types of unique relationships.

Step-father with step-daughter

#1 Have an opportunity to role model a positive fatherly influence

Your step-daughter may have a strong and healthy relationship with her own father, giving you an opportunity to reinforce her positive experience as a second positive male influence in her life. Or perhaps her dad is out of the picture. If so, check in with your partner (or your step-daughter, if it feels appropriate) – is there a desire for you to fulfil that role over time? And what sort of a relationship would you be comfortable with? Kids are perceptive and will pick up in an instant if your actions are misaligned to what you actually want, which isn't good for their sense of safety and security, and will inevitably cause you personal resentment. So, being clear about what she wants, and what role you would ideally like to authentically work towards with your step-daughter, will give you a goal to work consciously towards over time.

#2 Boundaries boundaries boundaries

Just like with any authority figure, step-fathers have a responsibility to consider the boundaries of the relationship with their step-daughter. Perhaps this is especially important given the historical cultural significance and care placed upon the contact between older 'stronger' male role models and arguably more vulnerable younger girls. This is true for physical boundaries, such as when it comes to appropriate contact (to hug or not to hug), and space – coming into bedrooms, for example, to say goodnight to older girls who might need a bit more privacy. It's also true for emotional boundaries, such as what subjects are on and off the table. Do check in with your own comfort levels here, and of course with your own partner to understand if there's anything in particular to avoid, or consider. But then you can take your cue from your step-daughter. As a general rule of thumb, when it comes to slightly more serious conversations over and above daily throwaway topics, allowing her to step forward and share/instigate things works well to ensure you are meeting her where she is.

#3 What opportunities do you have to bond?

Based on the circumstances, you may already have a good idea of which areas you are able to find common ground in. Perhaps these are activities you have started to do together since you and your partner moved in with one another, or conversations you find you both enjoy about subjects you find mutually interesting? Finding something that can become 'your thing' is a great way to establish the relationship in its own right. This could be a leisure activity that you do regularly, or it might be that you find ways to help her – building that photo wall in her bedroom, for example, or coming up with ways in which she can lend you some help, such as asking for her assistance in finding the perfect birthday gift for your partner.

Gaining my step-dad makes all the pain from my parents divorce worth it, and I would go through it all again just so I could have him as my step-dad. If I was to give some words of encouragement to anyone about to gain a step-parent, it would be that they may end up being one of the most beautiful, loving, supportive people in your life – so be open-minded. You are about to gain even more love.

Mia, step-daughter since her teens (36)

Step-mother with step-daughter

#1 Go easy on yourself, be patient

This has got to be one of the trickiest relationships to develop. As we've acknowledged, well in advance of the personal relationship between step-mother and step-daughter developing, this type of bond suffers from the weight of societal and cultural projections placed upon the step-mother archetype. Preconceptions exist and so the step-mother is almost starting from a negative position. Introductions are often met with foreboding, i.e. 'good luck meeting your new step-monster!', rather than with the neutral curiosity the step-father can enjoy, i.e. 'I don't know Mum's new boyfriend yet so can't judge, but he seems all right'. When researching, I lost count of the number of times I would say 'blended families' and the person I was in conversation with would say 'what are blended families – oh, you mean you're writing a book on wicked step-mothers?!' (and would go on to shudder). So it probably won't surprise you to learn that step-father figures often have a slightly easier ride than their female counterparts.

#2 Be sensitive to the child in you, as well as your step-daughter

You don't need to be a psychotherapist to know that if the parent(s) are a consistent and positive presence in their life, young girls generally form strong attachments to them, and are hyper-sensitive to the idea that something may threaten that. And rightly so. The parent-child relationship in its ideal form is sacred, and deserves to be protected and nurtured. These relationships form the foundational relationship we each have with the varied parts of ourselves that exist within us all, regardless of gender identity or biological sex.

However, the strength of this bond is often threatening to the young and vulnerable aspects of the step-mother's character, particularly when those aspects are not acknowledged or afforded care by either herself or her partner, and she feels disrespected or undermined in the household. This can leave the step-mother figure feeling hurt, pushed out and resentful. This is an understandable position, particularly if the step-mother had a difficult relationship with her own parent(s), or had a tricky experience in a previous blended family dynamic.

If this applies to you, it's a great idea to ensure you spend plenty of time all together as a new family unit, but do be proactive and support quality individual time between parent (your partner) and child. This will help ease the threat of isolation or abandonment that your step-daughter may experience, by showing you understand the need for their bond to continue in its own right. Step-parents, it's also entirely appropriate, if your partner's daughter is old enough, for your partner to ensure his/her daughter knows:

- Just how loved she is.
- Just how special their bond together is.
- That there is also room for the parent to invest in the newer bond they have with their partner (the step-parent).
- Most importantly . . . that while each separate relationship is important, they do not pose a threat to each other.

#3 Slow and steady

The step-mother/step-daughter relationship can become incredibly close and loving, but as with the relationships formed by the step-father, do take time to allow them to develop naturally, rather than force them. Your step-daughter may be desperate for a mother figure, and if that's the case, the dynamic may naturally present an easier opportunity for you to play a motherly role for her.

If she already enjoys a close and loving bond with her mum, she will be more inclined to want to protect and demonstrate loyalty towards her, and so it may take longer for a bond between you both to develop. This is entirely normal and something both you and your partner can be sensitive to. You don't need to spell out the fact you get it and are understanding, but if she does mention her mum, then encourage the conversation. If she mentions she feels disloyal, then you can gently explain that the heart is big enough to accommodate all the people in her life that are important to her. For as long as she wants it to be the case, her parents will occupy centre stage within it, but the heart can easily accommodate care and love for everyone that it needs to. Positive feelings simply don't work on a rations basis . . .

#4 Role modelling and advice

Look for common ground and pay attention to those areas you have a mutual interest in. Depending on custody arrangements and the age of your step-daughter, you may be asked to step in to an advisory and mentoring role – for example, to help her deal with the onset of puberty and the changes happening to her body. If your step-daughter has a good relationship with her own mother, then generally it makes sense to defer the honour of those conversations to mother and daughter, or perhaps her dad talks to her about this stuff as well as or instead? However, of course you can reinforce them when your step-daughter is staying with you where needed.

For those times when you are the only adult female role model around though, it can be a great opportunity to bond and establish a nurturing, caring relationship if your step-daughter indicates she needs a hand, or wants to learn about how to handle bodily changes.

This might happen even more naturally if you have teenage daughters of your own, and in that case you can consider whether to fold in your step-daughter to conversations you might have with them, to help her feel part of the dynamic.

I became a step-mum when my ex-husband's daughters were five and eight, and we went on to have two more girls together. This was an enriching experience for everyone; it was a privilege to be part of my step-daughter's lives in addition to my own children's. My step-daughters formed close bonds with their half-sisters, and my daughters benefit from having older sisters. With hindsight, though, I think the more difficult aspects were often sidestepped and left out, which meant thornier topics didn't get discussed or thought about. Part of what contributed to this was the fact my ex-husband avoided all conflict and difficult feelings in himself, as well as in those around him. However, in hindsight, I would have taken the lead and asked my step-daughters more questions and made more space for the difficult subjects.

Jasmine, step-mother and mother (50)

Step-father with step-son

#1 Patience is a virtue

Whether or not he already has sons, the step-father figure can often enjoy a slightly easier ride than their female counterpart when it comes to developing a relationship with their step-son(s). However, clearly this won't be the case for every dynamic – so, step-dads, if you're finding it tough going, then also be patient. If he's old enough, your step-son may feel protective of his mum, and may test you in ways he's not aware of. Make it clear you respect him and his relationship with his mum, which predated your own, and recognise it needs to be protected. Helpful messages (communicated explicitly or demonstrated implicitly) may include:

- You're not there to take over . . . there's a place for all of your relationships to flourish.
- You're simply there out of love . . . you don't pose a threat.
- You plan to stick around . . . consistency breeds security.

#2 Unleash your own inner child

Just like any adult, you, of course, have a kid inside you still – in therapy speak this is called your inner child. They can activate in moments of stress, but in happier, relaxed times they can come out to play and allow you to reconnect with your childhood self. Parents will already be familiar with this phenomenon, but if you're new to parenting through your blended family, then revel in it! This is your chance to introduce your step-son to all the things that made your heart sing when you were little – giggling over retro TV shows, playing laser tag or video games, baking cornflake cakes, helping him style his hair for the first time, camping in the garden. Whatever it is, whatever stage they're at . . . Have some fun and let your hair down.

#3 Role modelling and advice

This is pretty much a repeat of the above #4 in the previous section – your step-son may well have a close bond with their dad, and if they see them regularly will likely save sensitive conversations for them. But that won't be the case in every circumstance. For many reasons, you might end up spending more time with your step-son than he spends with his dad – perhaps Mum has majority custody? Which means, it may be you that's around for those 'firsts' and not their dad.

So, all I'll add is that your partner (their mum) may be just as likely to take the lead in conversations about puberty and other hormonal changes. This is because they have an existing bond with their son, and depending on the depth of the relationship you already enjoy with them, they may not feel ready to share such personal details with you. But . . . if they trust you enough to turn to you about this stuff, firstly get the green light from your partner to have these conversations. You are in a unique position over and above their mum who can understand what it's like to go through male puberty. So, if the opportunity presents itself, don't be afraid to step in and offer your step-son the guidance and advice he's looking for.

When Mum brought her new partner to live with the family, I was away at uni, and had been for some time, so I hadn't built the relationship with him that my younger sister/brother had by that point. I vividly remember coming home for the Christmas holidays to be introduced to him properly. He treated me like a grownup straight away – he didn't push the relationship too quickly, giving me space for things to develop at my pace, and demonstrated a respect for me. It really helped me feel comfortable around him. I like to think I'd take the same approach if I ever became a step-father too, and would definitely recommend it to others.

Peter, adult step-son (35)

Step-mother with step-son

This can be a great dynamic. Because the archetypal qualities of the mother figure are typically associated with the female, you may well over time become the go-to for helping to deal with practical care and the more emotional needs of your step-son(s). But take care in the relationship not to presume this is wanted or desired in the early stages. Your step-son may not feel he knows you well enough to be so vulnerable in front of you – and this may not even be needed in the household, especially if your partner is particularly close to him, and there is a close and loving bond between them. And like their sisterly counterparts, the sense of loyalty step-sons feel towards their own mothers may well slow down (at first) the development of the bond between you. Ultimately there are no wrongs or rights here, and if a motherly role is something you're open to playing during the times your step-son stays with you, then go for it. If you have no children of your own, this can be a wonderfully healing experience, and an opportunity to experience some of the joys of motherhood (of course, within the boundary of the 'step' relationship).

#Inclusivity and adaptation

If your own kids live with you all, it may mean your step-children will more readily accept you in a motherly role. However, while you will obviously parent your own kids, your step-son(s) may not be quite ready for you to kiss them goodnight and so on – you can still be sensitive to their need to belong and be part of the broader sibling group. Consider how you can adapt your approach to be inclusive, while not bombarding your step-kids with displays of emotional affection they may not be quite ready for.

#Embrace your role

In the scenario where you're not required to adopt a traditionally motherly role, then embrace it and have some fun! Whether you're reading bedtime stories, making up games to play, bonding over your love of chocolate cake, or helping them to choose their outfit for their school disco, this is all part of the memory-making process that will help to create and strengthen your long-term bond.

> I don't have any children of my own, but I am lucky enough to have a step-son. He's an absolute delight, and I am sure that what makes the whole dynamic easier is how much his dad encourages a positive relationship between us. It really helps that his mum (my husband's ex-wife) seems to be relaxed and happy that her ex has moved on with someone who is both good for him, and a positive influence on her son. My step-son and I find things to do together, not just with his dad around – although we're all about the team! – but we have developed lots of little 'in jokes' over the years, and things that

we like to do together. Having fun with him is something I take really seriously, and am blessed to be a part of his life.

Alison, step-mother (44)

And some general points to finish . . .

In many cases the step-child's drive to assuage their own difficult feelings can get in the way of developing a close bond with their step-parent(s). Feelings like guilt (e.g. for liking the step-parent figure), disloyalty (e.g. for perceiving they are abandoning the other parent in favour of the step-parent figure) or anger (e.g. for being asked to develop a close relationship with the step-parent figure they're not quite ready for).

The good news is that these difficult feelings do lessen with time, consistency and effort. However, in the meantime, they can easily be amplified if other people in the broader dynamic feel consciously or unconsciously threatened by these burgeoning bonds. For example, if the co-parent isn't quite ready to move on and expresses sorrow or anger towards the step-parent in front of the children . . . Or if grandparents express disapproval that their child's ex has moved on with another, in front of the children . . . When this happens, it can create setbacks for the step-parent/step-child relationship and the healthy development of the child's psyche that can sadly last for decades.

It's not either/or, it's more

Step-children simply have more people to learn from, to spend time with, to have fun with. The bottom line is, for each of these relationships to truly work, the mindset of abundance is a positive one to adopt. This means recognising that having additional role-models in the children's lives is ultimately healthy and positive. Children shouldn't need to have to decide that parent X is the only one who is available for conversations about schoolwork or puberty simply because of their gender, title or blood connection.

Children living in blended families have more choice, and should feel free to turn to whichever parent figure they feel can best fulfil their needs – or to turn to multiple parent figures if they want an extra perspective on the same topic. Parents can encourage this mindset by understanding and even making it clear they do not expect to be able to fulfil all of their children's needs all of the time. Even in nuclear families, it's very common for children to turn to one parent for one thing (e.g. emotional support), but to another for something different (e.g. professional guidance). Why should it be any different when step-parents are in the mix?

We also need to remember that our heart has enormous capacity – in fact, it's unlimited – for warm feelings of love, kindness and appreciation. In real terms, realising you have a high regard or a great deal of love for your step-father, say, changes absolutely nothing about the degree to which you may love and respect your own father.

> To be a step-parent you need a lot of patience, that's for sure. But all your love will be returned when the child is old enough to appreciate all that you have done, so have faith.
>
> *Nicole, adult step-daughter (30)*

Step aside for five
Conscious appreciation

Variant #1: If you are a step-child . . .

NB: Supportive adults can help teens with this exercise, or adult step-children could do this alone. It might be a little too sophisticated for young children to attempt, but you can share the principles of what we're working on in simpler terms – learning to see how the blended family dynamic is *additive* to their growth, rather than a substitute or attempt to erase the original and enduring bond between parent and child.

Consider the parents and step-parents in your life. On a piece of paper write each of their names down, with three rows underneath each one. Now have a think about the following:

> *In row one: Complete the sentence 'The qualities I value in X are . . .'*
> *In row two: Complete the sentence 'The things I (can) learn from X are . . .'*
> *In row three: Complete the sentence 'I turn to X for . . .'*

In each case, repetition of words/phrases for each of your parental figures is fine, but try to think of some unique things too, for each person.

The aim of this exercise is to notice and appreciate the fact that your parents and step-parents have some positive similarities in common, but also have unique qualities to offer; another positive aspect of our blended families in comparison to more traditional counterparts. In a successfully blended family there is an abundance of support and resources to meet all sorts of needs, whether they be practical, emotional, spiritual or psychological.

You do not need to worry that you have to choose, or that extra people in your life means you can no longer enjoy the same relationship and bonds that were already in place. Blended families mean more, not less. And in this case, more is definitely more!

Variant #2: For step-parents who may be struggling to bond with their step-children

The invitation here is to learn to consciously appreciate and value your step-children. However, if you have them, and you would like to include your own children in the exercise, then please feel free to.

On a piece of paper write the names of your step-children. Underneath each, complete the following three sentences:

In row one: 'The qualities I value in X are . . .'
In row two: 'The things I appreciate/admire most about X are . . .'
In row three: 'The kind of relationship I would like to have with X is . . .'

Again, repetition of words/phrases is fine here – no one needs to have a monopoly on kindness, for example.

The idea of this exercise is to help you see the positive strengths and qualities your step-children embody. By helping you to appraise them with fresh eyes, we start to lay the foundations that will help you realise the *potential* of your relationship.

Once you consider them as people in their own right – rather than what they may represent to you – it's much easier for positive bonds to develop.

8

How the Family Evolves

Now the family is established, let's consider the importance of the family group, and why it might be hard for some to be a part of one. We will look at some of the roles each member is given (or adopts); who is carrying what on behalf of the rest, who brings what emotional 'baggage' from previous experiences, and how that plays out in the rest of the group – for better or worse. Finally, we'll consider the sorts of practical roles blended family members take on.

Why groups are so powerful

Groups of people develop their own energy, which lives and breathes as a collective entity. The first groups we are generally a part of are known as our 'families of origin', and it is our experience of being part of this group that sets the stage for how we perceive other groups we are part of in the future – whether this be family constructs, teams in the workplace, study groups, sports teams, and so on.

Our experience of being part of a group includes things like to what degree we:

- Feel safe or unsafe
- Want to shine or hide
- Feel able to speak up or feel silenced
- Feel comfortable or uncomfortable
- Perceive ourselves (are we good/bad, likeable/unlikeable etc)

So, by the time we form our blended families, we are going to be bringing a lot of how we felt about our families of origin along for the ride. This is part of the rub of why it can feel so hard to be part of a blended family – but it's also what makes it so exciting.

You will have inevitably had difficult experiences within your family of origin, which the blended family can provide an opportunity to heal. Perhaps you never felt safe – and by this I don't mean physically unsafe, which is at the more extreme end of the scale. We can feel unsafe in all sorts of ways that can have a big impact on us as we grow older. An introvert living with a group of extroverts, for example, may well have felt regularly overwhelmed by the volume or vocalised needs of the collective energy of the others, and may have carried an innate sense of being different, not being understood, or not belonging, from childhood into adulthood.

By the same token, if you generally feel safe in groups, it can indicate you have been given great gifts by your family of origin – for example, the ability to speak your mind, a feeling of deep security, a strong sense of what it's like to be seen and noticed, or loved, how to deal with conflict healthily. When we feel secure, we have extra capacity to contribute effectively to the groups we are a part of. These gifts can be brought into your blended family dynamic to help others within it, who may not have had the privilege of learning these lessons early on.

Groups are made up of individuals

As well as having a think about what being part of a family group means to you, we can't avoid the fact that each group is made up of individuals, all of whom have their own characters and personalities, including emotional 'baggage', needs and desires, fears and concerns. Blended families should consider this as part of their healthy development. How you perceive individual family members will be affected by your prior experience of those you subconsciously associate with them, and will impact your behaviour towards them too.

Script formation

These experiences of both groups and individuals stay with us like relational imprints on our brains and bodies, and don't disappear with age, because we move away from our parents, or because we become a parent ourselves, or become estranged from a sibling, or because you divorced your spouse and met someone new. These relational imprints, which inform both how we relate to others and our perception of ourselves, form part of what we call our 'scripts'. We all have a script – it's like a blueprint of how to live and process information that we come across from an early age. Notice how our childhood experiences, whatever they may have been, often seem to be 'coincidentally' repeated in our adulthood. This is no coincidence – this is our 'scripts' playing out. So, unless we take the time to understand the one we have, the impact of it can be felt in the groups we are part of far into the future.

Once aware of our scripts, we can begin to take steps to challenge and then overcome them, by responding differently to the reality of the situations we find ourselves in, rather than continually 're-enacting' a situation we were previously unable to get out of.

Here are some examples of how our scripts, without any work to understand or process them, might negatively impact our experience of our blended families:

#1 As the youngest child, I was often not seen or heard or taken seriously – in my blended family, I often feel pushed aside.

#2 As the youngest child, I was used to lots of attention – in my blended family, I often crave the limelight.

#3 In my family of origin, I was often shamed by an aggressive father – in my blended family, I was instantly scared of my step-father, who seemed to be just like Dad.

#4 In my family of origin, I was the eldest child and expected to help out a lot – in my blended family, I find everyone seems to dump on me.

#5 When my parents separated, my step-mum came on the scene and made it clear she didn't like me and didn't seem to want me to have a relationship with my dad. In my blended family today, I often feel as if my partner deprioritises me in favour of his daughter.

#6 I've got five siblings and was constantly excluded. When Dad remarried and introduced us to his partner's three children, I instantly knew the same thing was going to happen again and dreaded meeting them.

These examples are a good first step – by talking through what it was like then and now, we start to make important links between our earlier experience, and notice how they can impact our present.

Using some fresh examples, let's now consider the kind of transformation that might be possible when we start to challenge our scripts proactively and take action, which is one step further on from simply making the link:

#1 This: You have been part of what can only be described as an abusive relationship with your partner, and every time you try to leave you find yourself getting sucked back in.

Becomes: You confront yourself with the fact you have remained in a relationship with an abusive boyfriend because you were unconsciously trying to prove yourself to the father who abandoned you. The constant rejection from your partner was reinforcing the belief your inner child carried of not being lovable, which you now realise was not true at all. When you realise this, you leave the relationship, because the adult in you knows you deserve better. You are much happier.

#2 This: Your wife seems to make all of the decisions, which most of the time you're happy to accept, but you recognise, over the years, it's completely disempowered you and you worry you're too far gone to make a change.

Becomes: You realise you have been expecting your partner to make all the decisions because you had a domineering mother who insisted on running the household with what felt like an 'iron grip'. So, you sit down with your wife and tell her about your discovery. She is overcome with relief – at times being responsible for making all the decisions has felt like a huge burden. She felt resentful that you leave everything to her, but didn't know how to talk to you about it. You feel optimistic and together you discuss how to share decision making out between you. You are both much happier, the relationship feels safer and more satisfying.

#3 This: You wish you were closer to your step-sister, but maybe there's just not much of a connection. It makes you sad, but maybe you just need to accept this is how it will always be.

Becomes: You realise you were in fierce competition with your own sister as you were growing up, which led to a lot of conflict between the two of you. But as a result, you've been keeping your new step-sister at arms length, and she has repeatedly made it clear she wants to get to know you. So you consciously begin to forge a closer relationship with her and find that she, having never had a sibling of her own growing up, was just really happy to finally have a brother figure in her life. The more you get to know her, you realise you don't need to compete, and she is very much her own person. You develop a close bond. You are much happier.

I wonder what changes you would like to make if you became aware of and challenged your own script?

Step aside for five
Family scripts

Let's have a look at how your experiences of being part of a family in the past may be affecting your experience of your blended family today. For the most benefit, it is ideal if each of the adult members of the blended family complete this exercise separately. As we've acknowledged, the blended family needs all of the adult minds within it to be thinking consciously about how it runs in order to create best results, as you can't be expected to do all of the work on behalf of everyone. However, if it is just you doing this, then don't be deterred – personal development work is always beneficial, and additive to the groups we are a part of.

So, grab your journal and ask yourself the following questions about the family you grew up in. In your childhood, you may have had multiple experiences of being part of a family, depending on what age you were if and when your parents separated. So, simply write about the experiences that stand out.

Looking back:
What did it feel like to be part of your family of origin?

What did you learn about yourself by being a part of it? Were you continually expected to fulfil a particular role?

What did you learn about being a part of a group?

The present:
What is the dynamic like in your current blended family? In what ways does the present dynamic remind you of the families you used to be a part of? This might be about the group overall, or it might be about a particular member of it that you feel particularly close to or wary of.

Is this based on reality, or is it possible your perception might somehow be connected to your prior experience? How do you know the difference?

What skills and qualities do you have that you already bring to your blended family? Do you feel safe and valued enough to use them? If not, do you have insight as to why?

Looking ahead:
How would you like the family dynamic to evolve, grow

closer? What does it need more of or less of? How can you contribute to that?

How can the blended family you are a part of help you to overcome any fears or concerns or other negative energy you carry about your past experiences?

Do you have any skills and qualities that are yet to emerge in the family dynamic? What would it take for you to be able to showcase them?

Now you're equipped with a little more self awareness, and have done some work on what you might be bringing to proceedings, let's turn our attention to the rest of the family, and take a closer look at some of the roles people may be occupying without anyone realising.

Here are some common ones to have a think about, and here we're going to borrow a couple of well trodden theory paths to illustrate the points, beginning with the drama triangle, the brainchild of Stephen Karpman. The drama triangle comprises three roles: rescuer, victim and persecutor.

Rescuer

Our rescuer is the one who constantly rides in to save the day, to be useful, and fix the problems of others ... even when people don't need saving or fixing. The rescuer has great intentions, but in order for them to rescue, it means they are setting someone else up in the family to be the persecutor or the victim, and this can cause frustration and resentment for those around.

Victim

Roll up, roll up, the family victim. This person is constantly down-trodden, losing out because of everyone else's bad behaviours, and can believe the world is against them. The victim wants to be looked after and cared about, which is important, but in order for them to try to get what they want, this behaviour means someone else is again put into the role of attacker, and someone else again is relied upon to 'rescue'. Plus, for our victim, this tendency has the added benefit of deflecting away any responsibility they might have in the relational dynamic – the wide-eyed 'don't look at me, I didn't do anything . . .' narrative is also infuriating to witness!

Persecutor

Finally, step forward our persecutor. This one is constantly put in the frame for causing trouble. They are often the truth seeker, wanting justice, and not afraid to call out what they see as negative behaviours, but are branded with the 'outspoken' or 'rude' brush.

We all occupy each of these roles from time to time – and that's okay. There is generally good intentions beneath each of the behaviours, as you have read; all behaviour has a purpose. The human motivations to be seen, to seek justice and truth, and hold people responsible for their actions, and to protect those we see as weaker, are powerful and drive our behaviours.

Sometimes people are genuinely wronged, and it can be incredibly empowering for them to feel safe enough to speak up and be listened to.

Sometimes people are genuinely defenceless, and benefit from additional support, protection or loyalty from other family members.

Sometimes people can lash out and use angry words and body language to punish someone, which can be seen as fair or unfair, depending on the situation.

But no one can always be the victim, no one is for ever the aggressor, and we know that putting yourself in the role of rescuing others is not only draining, but often means you forget to look after your own needs.

The trouble with the drama triangle is that it activates when we are *unconsciously* handed these roles by other family members, and thereafter are perceived to be continually acting them out without conscious thought as to whether this is actually true. We can also put ourselves into these positions, *unconsciously* behaving in such a way in an *unconscious* attempt to resolve the woundings of our own childhoods. This is one of the ways our brain tries to make sense of all the information we have in our day-to-day life, which would be far too difficult to sift through consciously. So we ourselves start to default to particular 'go to' positions, and we make lazy assumptions about how we perceive others. This is problematic, as it may not be our truth, and it can be disempowering – the victim becomes the 'boy who cried wolf', whom people stop listening to or taking seriously. The attacker becomes the trouble maker. The rescuer becomes irritating, and can be seen as a martyr to someone else's cause.

This is reductive. It stops us responding to each situation appropriately, and we cast judgements about family members before taking the time to try to understand what's really going on in the dynamic. We both ask questions and see with eyes from an inherently biased position. We stop believing that the attacker is sometimes the victim, we buy into the fact our rescuer is incapable of being mean or behaving badly, and we start to believe our victims need to be wrapped in cotton wool.

Have a think about your blended family, and see if you can answer these questions:

- Can you spot who is taking on each role?
- Can you see familiar patterns emerging?
- How have you been contributing to it?
- Are you a little more aware of what role you tend to take on?
- And, most importantly, now that you spot it, what can you start to do to 'get off the drama triangle' and help each dynamic be seen for what it is?

Next up is the work of Eric Berne, who developed a theoretical concept called the PAC model, contributing to a branch of therapy called Transactional Analysis. The acronym stands for one of three 'ego states' we can occupy from time to time: Parent, Adult and Child. Each member of the blended family can all occupy each one of these states, regardless of their age or position in the household, and we generally move fluidly from position to position as we respond to our own needs and adapt to our perceptions of those around us.

Parent state

Those in 'parent' mode show up in a few different ways, some of which are welcomed in the household while others will be grating:

When someone is occupying 'nurturing parent', they might take on a caring role when someone is sick or struggling. When we've had a tough day at work, and turn to our partner for support, we typically want them to be in their 'nurturing parent' state when they respond.

When someone is in a 'controlling parent' state, on the other hand, they might be perceived as bossy; perhaps taking over and assuming responsibility for things that others would want to take on, given the opportunity. They delegate tasks in authoritarian fashion, set controls over spending limits or make all the decisions about household purchases, for example.

The position of parent can also be adopted and weaponised during conflict, by someone unwilling to take responsibility for how they're feeling, e.g. they're hurt or vulnerable. Instead of the very adult position of 'Okay, we're both upset here – let's take a moment and share what's going on for both of us, so we can help to make it better', the language turns into something altogether more confrontational, i.e. 'Come back to me when you are ready to have a grown-up conversation – you're behaving like a child!' We call this type of parental behaviour the 'critical parent'.

Adult state

The 'adult' state of mind is the part that takes the reins when we are feeling calm and secure, and is regarded as a healthy and secure position to occupy. This is the place from which we make our best decisions. Generally, these behaviours are perceived as positive, healthy and helpful – someone in their adult state can help to mediate, provide a balanced view, and be relied upon to be 'sensible'.

Sometimes, however, children learn to become overly adult from far too young an age – 'growing up too soon' if, for example, their parents themselves are dealing with practical constraints, like reduced physical capacity, or because of psychological or emotional immaturity. This presents a challenge for the child as the inherent joy, innocence and playful nature within becomes buried underneath the assumed and perhaps false maturity of the adult they think they *need* to be in order to be safe or accepted. We call this the 'parentified child'.

Parentified children often feel they are not good enough because their own needs weren't noticed or looked after appropriately, and they can also feel they are to blame for everything – so used are they to having to take responsibility for the grownups around them.

Child state

It can feel great to regress to a child state as an adult – this can happen very appropriately and helpfully in the blended family dynamic. Regression can be really healing, offering contentment and safety. Playing games . . . accessing mischief and joy through playing pranks and messing around together . . . feeling cosy and warm when festive food is made in the holidays . . . allowing yourself to be comforted if you're hurt or injured.

Issues arise, however, when the adult regresses to a child state as a result of feeling unsafe or insecure. Unhelpful behaviours can emerge, such as petulance, emotional withdrawal, and/or an insistence things be done a certain way (imagine a toddler having a tantrum).

We also recognise what we call an 'adaptive child', through a tendency to people please, perhaps altering/changing a point of view or behaviour in order to fit in with others around us. And as we saw above, adults can very much be unwittingly put into a 'child' state position by another member of the household, who in trying to feel superior in the household (e.g. to try and win an argument) has adopted the state of 'parent'.

So, in summary, we naturally become the parent or the child at times, responding automatically to our environments. The key is to adopt each position as consciously and congruently as possible. For conflict to be resolved in our blended families, and in all relationships, we want to try to ensure that all adults in the household can do this from their 'adult positions', and to encourage age-appropriate responses to difficult situations. To do this, we observe our own behaviour and whether we have a 'go-to position' that we turn to when stressed, which might originate from our experiences at a much younger age. Then we consider how we are both enabling positive behaviours, and holding a mirror up to the negative actions of others.

Practical roles

Dividing up practical household roles in a blended family is not dissimilar to any other family construct, in that who does what comes down to time, capacity and competency. However, what sets the blended family apart is the particular significance tasks represent for the individual, based on their prior experience.

Prior association

When new couples form after divorce or separation, it's a chance to begin afresh and redress previous dynamics that one or both members found challenging in their previous relationships. For example, an expectation for one person to take care of the cooking when they didn't particularly like it, or a demand for one to do the school run because of their preference to be close to the children (denying their partner of the opportunity in the process), or another's desire to prioritise their career. This is a really positive aspect of a blended family, and one that can be healing for the couple, who get to decide consciously what's right for them.

I've known fathers take pleasure in suddenly, as a result of marital separation, needing to take a lot more responsibility for childcare because, in their previous nuclear family dynamic, domestic labour was divided into more traditional gender-based roles (i.e. the female takes care of majority of childcare). I've known women begin to find joy in cooking regularly, because in their previous relationship their partner was a chef and territorial about sharing the cooking duties at home. And for those who come to the blended family dynamic from living a single or single-parent lifestyle, it can be incredibly gratifying to suddenly have another adult to share stuff with.

What about task division among the kids?

Kids bring further layers to consider. Where both members of the couple have children, those children may well have had different levels of responsibility placed upon them by their parents at the same age, before the blended family existed. One may have been expected to make their own bed . . . another might have been used to making themselves breakfast . . . Others will have been taught that pocket money or allowances are only handed out when cars are washed or dishwashers loaded etc, while their step-siblings enjoyed their pocket money with no conditions attached. You can see the differences that arise, and their potential for conflict. To create a harmonious dynamic, then, the blended family ideally needs to navigate towards a place where the same expectations are placed upon each child in the blended household, to avoid unnecessary conflict and feelings of resentment building up – between both children and the adults.

At first, when you're aligning expectations, conflict might arise as people adjust to being given more responsibility. However, being consistent and ensuring both members of the couple are empowered and relied on to reinforce these expectations will mean the new family routines are adopted more quickly.

Where your young adults or teens resent additional domestic responsibilities, you'll perhaps deal with the frustration of the step-brother/sister in the household who has already been used to doing X or Y task for some time. Perhaps they start to challenge the jobs they're allotted, or become irritated by the perceived laziness of their step-sibling. However, you can view this as an issue for the collective – i.e. the whole household.

Everyone has responsibility, and therefore if one person isn't pulling their weight it affects the broader dynamic. So, it would be appropriate in these circumstances to sit down together and reset expectations. Outlining the tasks each person has responsibility for (including the adults), ensuring everyone is aware of their roles. You may find there is a lack of knowledge or awareness, which provides opportunity for clarification. Where there is still a sense of unwillingness, you can explore that and either find a healthy compromise if you discover there is a reasonable explanation as to *why* one is resistant to take responsibility for a particular task, or you can gently reinforce why it's important.

What each task signifies for the family and members within it

As blended families begin to integrate, the division of labour changes, particularly if new members join an existing household. For example, an incoming step-parent may begin to take on some responsibility for running the household, and this in many cases extends to helping to look after the children. The blended couple can talk about what's right for them, and here it's important for assumptions not to be made on either side.

For example, doing the school run may be seen as a necessary chore for the parents, which they don't want to impose on their partner. For childless step-parents, however, the prospect of having that responsibility may be an honour, signifying a deepening level of trust and a chance to take some responsibility for the childcare, providing an opportunity to bond with their prospective step-children.

Alternatively, where the parent may have assumed the school run would be equally divided, or even fall to the incoming step-parent once they moved in (e.g. based on historical gender norms, or the routine in the previous nuclear dynamic), the step-parent may have a very different idea. Perhaps, for them, their career is important and while keen to get stuck into the family dynamic, they very much see that sort of responsibility as the domain of the parent. Or perhaps they had assumed that taking responsibility for tasks such as this would be limited only to their own children?

The point here is that, in the blended family, for things to work there has to be conscious communication between the adults. It's so easy to make assumptions, but you have formed a new dynamic which deserves fresh consideration so you can build your ideal lifestyle together. The fresh start you are both signing up to simply does not need to be dictated by the norms and rituals of the prior relationships/marriages each of you have come from.

> When my partner moved in, my mindset was: These are my children, and the childcare burden shouldn't impact her (although she was willing to help). So, at first, I tried to do everything, but as the saying goes 'many hands make light work', and where appropriate I now accept the offer of support. I think as long as you don't look at your partner as a childcare solution, and take them for granted, then letting them help as much as they are willing to is a good thing. Not only does it make my life easier, but it also enables a chance for one-to-one time with

> my kid(s) and my partner, so they can create their own bond.
> It's also the small things that matter too – for example, I also
> ensure I thank her for helping out every time, so she knows
> I'm appreciative.
>
> *Harry, parent (47)*

Allowing everyone to take responsibility

When contributing to the household, everyone in the family is going to have a list of things they are naturally good at, as well as their preferences. One of the most common gripes that I come across is the way that everyday practical tasks, such as shopping, washing, cooking and cleaning, are shared out among newly blended families.

Younger children might have light expectations delegated to them, such as making their bed in the morning, or popping dirty clothes in a laundry basket. But where there are older children/teens/young adults involved, could you talk through who would like to take responsibility for what? You might love cooking, but if your twenty-year-old step-son is at catering college and wants to show you all what he can do, allowing him to take responsibility for the cooking on set nights each week will give everyone else a break. It will also empower him, and allow him to show off his skills. Looking at these sorts of tasks not as a set of chores that we learn to resent by word association, but as a chance to contribute and help, contributes to the smooth running of the blended family.

Resentment within the blended couple and what to do about it

Either half of the couple may feel a little powerless in the dynamic at times, and often the step-parent figure is the one to feel it. This may be the case for a number of reasons:

- One person has joined the rest of the family in their physical space (the home the parent shares with the kids) and so feels it's not their right to set boundaries etc.
- Step-children resent the incoming step-parent.
- The step-parent's experience in a previous blended family has made them fearful about history repeating itself.

However, there is another phenomenon we need to address, which is how energy is exchanged within the couple, and how this affects the blended family.

In previous chapters, we looked at the impact of guilty feelings, and this more often than not in our blended family centres around the guilt the parent has taken on, as a consequence of things like:

- The ending of their previous relationship.
- Leaving the nuclear family home.
- Fearing these actions will have a negative impact on the children's psyche as a result.

Often, this results in a dynamic where the parent finds it harder to discipline their children or set boundaries and set expectations for the respect that should be afforded to the step-parent. When this occurs, remember that any system strives for balance, and this often happens unconsciously. So if the parent tends to adopt a more passive approach, the step-parent will often take on the more active feelings and position, in an unconscious attempt to restore balance. This might be verbally expressed, and may result in arguments if the parent isn't willing to address what might be going on for them – or it might be unexpressed, resulting in simmering resentment.

The solution here is for the more passive adult (the parent, in this case) to try to understand the root cause of their passivity. What's stopping them from allowing their child(ren) to take age-appropriate responsibility for their lives, what holds them back from helping their child(ren) to understand the impact of certain words or behaviours in the household, and what role have they been putting the step-parent in as a result?

We know the step-parent becomes the scapegoat in this dynamic – the hard, strict one, who is put into the position of the aggressor (hello, drama triangle). The child consequently becomes the victim, and the parent neatly takes on the rescuing role. Which is convenient, as the parent can soothe themselves and avoid dealing with their own guilty feelings, the children have an easy, more 'acceptable' place to put their feelings of anger or disdain, and consequently, no growth (which, as we know, takes time and effort) needs to happen. And for our step-parent, particularly over time, resentment starts to build.

It's important to highlight the role of the parent, because it is often overlooked in blended family dynamics, and all the emotional and psychological responsibility to ensure things are harmonious is handed to the step-parent. Which, as we know, is sadly a narrative that is often easy to settle on, as it is culturally and societally re-inforced with archetypal expectations of the step-parent in all their supposed 'wickedness'.

The step-parent, of course, has *just as much* responsibility to consider their own behaviours, and ensure that their own past woundings aren't affecting the level of care and respect they show to their step-children. And step-parents often do not behave well.

But by the same token, often *parents* do not behave well. So the key here is to appraise each dynamic for what it is, and try not to let broader archetypal constructs and your own *past* experiences get in the way of you consciously taking a look at what's going on in your own family in the *here and now*.

In the most successful blended families, the parent takes *equal* responsibility for their impact and role in the blended family, alongside the step-parent. They take care to set expectations for how their partner deserves to be treated, and they take care to not let their own uncomfortable feelings get in the way of actively parenting their children.

When we met each other, we both quickly heard about how hard our previous marriages had been; we hadn't felt respected, and there was lots of tension. So when we got together, we revelled in the things we both loved to do that had caused friction in our previous dynamics (both of us are active for example). We were probably overly respectful of each other to begin with, as we had both been used to our former partners getting their own way. But that strong appreciation for one another is one of the best things about our relationship today, years later, and has made it all so much easier as we've come together as a family, divvying up responsibilities and managing our household. We talk about everything, we don't assume our own preferred way of doing something is best, and we feel safe and confident enough to share our own views.

Rich and Joanna, parents and step-parents (late 30s)

9

Strengthening Your Blended Family

This chapter is dedicated to long-established blended families. Over time, they have evolved with co-created values, norms, and rituals, so now, the family likely feels safe. This creates space to reflect on what it stands for and to embrace nostalgia and sentiment as memories and traditions start to build up.

Family values

If I asked you what your values were, would you know off the top of your head? My guess is no. For most people, values are something which are lived automatically rather than thought about consciously. If shown a list of values, however, I would also hazard a guess that most people would be able to choose some that resonated. Our values are important, as they help to govern our behaviour and inform the way in which we perceive others.

In the workplace, it's not uncommon for businesses to define the company values – which often are a source of derision internally. While they exist on paper, they aren't followed every day by every employee. And, of course, this is because it's often hard to do in practice. We're all human, we live our lives at a million miles an hour, we make mistakes, we get frustrated, and none of us show up at our best when we're tired, stressed or preoccupied. But when done well by an organisation, values are reinforced at every available opportunity – people are hired by the extent they fit and exude the values, they become a way of defining and setting standards for behaviour, and they can influence many things, such as company strategy, customer activity and HR policies. The values literally form the fabric of the organisation.

So what does all this have to do with our blended families?

All families have their own collective rhythm, personality and style. But unlike a nuclear family, the blended family has formed when at least one of the adults within it has had some experience of creating a family unit in their adulthood previously. So as we saw in Chapter Eight, each adult brings to bear their experience from their family of origin, as well as from adulthood. Everyone will have a slightly different view as to what's important, what they need from the others, and in what sort of environment they can thrive. So, here is a fresh chance for our blended family to consider their collective values, and how they want to live with one another. It's a great opportunity to build a sense of teamwork and camaraderie to ensure everyone feels safe, and takes pride in being part of it.

Defining values can help not only to set up the family for a shared understanding, but they can also help to reset a maturing family dynamic, where bad habits have formed and resentments may have started to creep in.

Family motto

Similarly, let's look at family mottos. Lots of old families that have passed traditions from generation to generation have a family motto. It's generally a small sentence that is easy to remember, acting as a guiding mission for each family member to follow. Those that have them are often proud the one they belong to stands for something; the sense of history and tradition can be powerful, helping people to feel safe on a deep and meaningful level.

Mottos can be easily learned by everyone in the family, including young children.

The family motto is a fantastic way to create shared understanding and a sense of belonging among the blended family. It can set the family apart and create a sense of kinship that can help to bond the blended family together by creating conscious ties – which can be helpful, particularly in the absence of biological ties.

How important is timing?

In a moment, we're going to look at how you can create a set of values and a motto for your blended family. Before we do, however, let's have a think about timing. It's a tricky one – introduce it too early and it may feel contrived or inauthentic.

Particularly in the very early stages, people may well not be ready to consider themselves part of a new blended family – preferring instead to think of things in much more simple terms, such as 'Mum has a new partner', or 'Daddy has met someone special'. If that's where you're at in your blended family, the time likely hasn't come yet when either of these exercises will be appropriate. On the other end of the scale, if you've all been living together for years, it might seem a bit odd to suddenly introduce them!

Therefore, only you and your partner will be able to judge the nuance of when this is right for your family. As a loose guide, perhaps you've been living together for around a year, at a point when you could describe each relationship as established. Perhaps they are also relatively harmonious. It will be hard, to say the least, to do something like this when one or more of the dyads (a relationship between two people within the blended family, e.g. step-mum and step-son) are dysfunctional, or have broken down altogether.

Step aside for five
Creating your blended family motto and set of values

These are two fun exercises that can be done to help the maturing blended family dynamic flourish. Everyone in the family can join in – you get to make each one as fun and interactive as you like, unleashing your creative side!

Exercise #1: Blended Family Motto

Step 1 – Sitting down together, first have a conversation so everyone knows what the task is and why you're doing it. You might need to explain to the smaller ones what a motto is.

Step 2 – Give everyone a piece of paper and a pen. Set the timer for five minutes and give everyone an opportunity to write their ideas down for what the family motto should be. A quick internet search will give you plenty of ideas for inspiration if people are stuck.

Step 3 – Go around the table and give everyone an opportunity to share what they've written with the rest of the family. It's important to also encourage people to explain how they came up with their ideas, as this might provide some food for thought for the motto you all end up agreeing on. While this process is happening, get everyone to make notes of particular words or parts of each suggestion that resonate with them.

Step 4 – Shortlist favourite suggestions, and get everyone to contribute to the discussion by sharing what was written on their notes lists, adding in or substituting words that offer particular meaning and resonate more with the others. Finalise what feels right for everyone. The important thing is to ensure everyone has a voice and is able to share their ideas. As with most things, the journey here is just as important as the destination. This activity is a bonding activity designed to bring you even closer together, and honour the relationships you have worked so hard to build – which are only going to grow stronger.

Step 5 – With the finished article, decide if and how you want to represent it around the house. Getting personalised prints produced and framed, or having bespoke hanging signs produced are easily achieved these days – or you could write it on cards. And if you want to go even further . . . I've even known it to be tattooed onto the body.

Exercise #2: Blended Family Values
Step 1 – Begin with you all around the table, each armed with some pen and paper. If available, also stick a much larger piece of paper onto a wall so you can all see.
Step 2 – Ask everyone to draw some objects and symbols that

represent the family when it's at its best, what you want your family to be known for. For example, someone might draw a heart indicating it would be caring, or a laughing face emoji to show the importance of having fun together. If you want to get even more creative, you could give people categories to do this with – for example, fruit or animals.

Step 3 – Each person can then share their drawings with the rest of the group, and explain why they chose each particular one. While this is happening, on the big piece of paper someone can write down each of the adjectives that are used to describe each object – e.g. honest, trustworthy, kind, playful.

Step 4 – Get each person to vote, by marking the words that resonate the most. I'd suggest settling on between four and six, simply choosing the ones with the highest number of votes.

When too many values are defined, no one can remember them and they get forgotten, so less is often more.

Step 5 – Once you have finalised your family values, as a finishing touch you could define how you're each going to try to live them throughout the year. Let's say 'kindness' ended up on the list. One person might commit to making someone a cup of tea in the mornings . . . Another might help someone else with their homework . . . And so on. Each person will end up with a really nice list of positive acts they feel they can do easily. Maybe you could think of consequences for people who don't 'live' the family values (a little bit like the concept of a swear jar).

These exercises exist for a moment in time, and of course in an ideal world the effects of them will be felt for years to come. But what about the everyday moments that happen unexpectedly, that have a profound impact on one or more of the family group? How can these moments be captured and recognised as an opportunity to lay down new traditions and rituals that the whole family can carry out regularly.

We do these things naturally in the other groups we are a part of. We have 'in jokes', and little bonding moments that we share with close friends. Then there are the particular things we say when we greet particular people, or little actions that we undertake, such as a special handshake. Things are no different in a blended family. These things tend to bubble up organically, and they will evolve over time as the family connection and each inter-family relationship within it deepens. The invitation with a blended family, however, is to be really conscious of each of these moments. In the earlier stages you may want to suggest things to do together as a family unit. Before long these ideas will be repeated, and everyone in the family will begin to look forward to them, building on the initial ritual and adding little touches that signal how engaged everyone is, and committed to making memories together.

Why be so conscious of it? And why does it matter so much in a blended family? Well, as we have seen, there is lots of room for tension and difficulties, with all the conflicting feelings that characterise this type of group, particularly in the early stages. In addition, when there are lots of different personalities converging in a newly formed household, it can take a little while before people feel they've found their voice and truly 'belong'.

A bit of conscious effort, therefore, especially from the adults, to build sentiment, have fun, and develop rituals to celebrate life or seasonal events, can be important to help everyone settle. It can also be a way to live the values you set out, by using those sentiments to guide how you interact regularly and bond. Like this:

The value is . . . Having fun.

Your action could be . . . to plan in an annual trip to a theme park

The value is . . . Sharing successes.

Your action could be . . . at the end of every week over dinner, ask everyone to share their highlight from the week, and make a Big Deal of it.

The value is . . . To spend time with each other every week.

Your action could be . . . a weekly family movie night.

Each family member will, of course, bring with them memories of rituals that were created in a previous family, which the kids might still experience in your co-parent's household. The adults in the blended family should avoid replicating special moments/rituals the children already share with another parent. Some of the basics, though, may be unavoidable – let's say the children are staying with you and your partner on their birthday, and you both want to make a cake for them. While this may be something their other parent also does, there is no issue with them having two, one for each house. It's actually a lovely thing that the child has multiple people in their lives who want to celebrate with them and mark the occasion. On the other hand, if the kids share with you that when they go to stay with their mum/dad, every weekend they all have snuggle time in bed and watch something together before having pancakes for breakfast – be prepared to encounter some resistance if you suddenly introduce exactly the same routine!

While your intent is great, given the specificity of the ritual, the kids will unavoidably be reminded of their other parent, and they may feel a heightened sense of divided loyalty, begin to miss them, feel guilty, or compare experiences. It's also important not to *consciously* undermine the rituals the children might become accustomed to in their other parent's household. As we've seen with the birthday cake example above, there might be some unavoidable overlap in some cases – but by and large try and focus on creating your own unique experiences the kids can get used to and enjoy, guilt-free.

So far here we have focused on the importance of ritual, as well as the identity of the blended family. This is a really rewarding element and I'm confident that if you can pay attention to these sorts of things from the beginning, you will stand the best possible chance of building something really special. But the danger zone of focusing solely on this sort of thing is that we *idealise* the family unit – it's all sunshine and skipping through meadows, which we know is simply not realistic!

Just like any other type of group, ruptures occur and we experience differences of opinion from time to time. In our efforts to repair, sometimes we get it right first time . . . but more often than not we learn from our mistakes.

So, another exercise to try as a family, if you are up for the challenge – and only once the dynamic has existed for a while – is to undertake a little review. A review will mean different things to different people. For some this will be nothing more than a quick chat every few months while driving to the supermarket. For others it might be a nightly debrief at everyone's favourite time of day for 'deep and meaningfuls' . . . Bedtime! In couples therapy, we sometimes call it a MOT or a Health Check. Each approach has its place, and of course you can spend as much time as you want on yours. But, for those who want to consciously and carefully take a look at the group and check in, then you could consider something a little more . . . robust. Try this for size:

Step aside for five
Blended family review

The purpose of the review is to, metaphorically speaking, brush the blended family's hair. If it's a bit knotty, or not shiny anymore, you can see this as an opportunity to air any grievances, recconnect and reset. The result should be a mane of smooth shiny locks that Pantene would be proud of (again, I realise that's an idealistic point, but I'm hoping you get my drift). If you're all getting along brilliantly, and there are no issues, then you perhaps don't need to go to these lengths (pun not intended). However, there's always room to make things better.

For this exercise to work, both members of the blended couple are going to need to be relatively self-aware, and invested in optimising the blended family dynamic. The couple need to be pulling their weight and operating as a team, otherwise you will each unwittingly undermine the point of the exercise.

You can try this with as many of the family as possible. If there is any kind of friction or knotty dynamics you're hoping to iron out with this, then the member of the blended couple who is the most 'neutral' could be the one to instigate it.

Plan it on a day where no one is working, as a) no one wants to be ambushed at the end of a long working day, when people are preoccupied and tired, and b) time to plan means people know what they're walking into, and can have a think about what they'd like to say.

When you talk to other family members about it, you don't need to say the words 'review'. For many it will have formal connotations, especially if you are used to annual performance reviews in your workplace. Instead, you could use terms like 'Family MOT'. Or simply share that you're all going to get together to have a chat about the family, and iron out a couple of things that have happened recently, or figure out how you can all be a bit happier together.

Do include the whole of the blended family, if you can, and if it's appropriate. This might mean adult children who no longer live in the blended family home – away at university, for example. If adult children have moved in with their partners, then invite the partner along too. The point is that this should be an inclusive conversation. A member of a family is a member of the family – and turning twenty-five or moving in with a girlfriend/boyfriend doesn't suddenly mean the adult child should be excluded. Especially if the adult child still has much younger siblings or half-siblings who still live with the blended couple.

Gather around the table – in my house this would be accompanied by tea and cake to help the process along (it's lemon drizzle if you're asking). Start by explaining how important the family is to you both, and hopefully everyone else too. Then share the purpose of getting together, and find your own words for this that resonate with everyone – not everyone will appreciate hair brushing analogies, more's the pity.

In professional contexts, we often use a tool called 'stop, start, continue'. It's simple and everyone can join in. The issue people sometimes have with this is that it becomes a bit of a box-ticking exercise – everyone has good intentions, but often the really juicy stuff that people are seriously bothered about doesn't get raised. Or, if it does, it can get swept under the carpet. In addition, because in a professional context there are often many more people doing an exercise like this, it can be hard to really follow up on everyone's suggestions. So what started as a good opportunity for growth can turn into what feels a bit like a waste of time.

However, this is different!

- Your blended family means the world to you and your partner.
- No one wants to live in an unhappy or friction-filled home – so you and your partner should be fairly motivated for this to go well.
- Your family will fit round the table, so it should (in theory anyway!) be a little easier to hear what everyone has to say, find solutions and achieve consensus. Versus a room full of forty people all saying different things.

Let's use a simple three part review framework as the basis for this exercise:

Give everyone some sticky notes and a pen.

Part #1 Continue:
Ask each person to think about

a. Some of the elements they really appreciate about the family as a whole.
b. Some things that individuals in the family do in

particular that are appreciated and noticed. These might be big things or small things – everything is welcome.

Then go around the table and ask everyone to share what they've written. This is the good stuff, a chance to feel good and compliment each other – so don't hold back!

Part #2 Stop

This is the opportunity for people to have a think about things that might be happening that they find a bit difficult, upsetting, or annoying.

a. Invite people to share things that relate to the family as a whole
b. Also invite people to have a think if there is anything that's happening between them and just one other member of the family. It's okay to name those things too.

Again, go around the table and get everyone to share what they thought of what's been said. This bit of the exercise is a nice way to practise basic conflict resolution, and in some ways the younger the kids are the better – it's never too early to start instilling a healthy way to air frustrations and resolve basic issues. It's ideal if everyone has at least one or two things to say, so everyone gets a turn to air something that's been niggling them.

Try to encourage people to name the 'thing' that they find challenging, and in doing so keeping as much of the focus as possible on the impact it has. This will help the people on the receiving end think about what they might want to do differently, as it's always easier to hear when the focus isn't on the person on the receiving end of the feedback. Let's look at a quick example.

Example A
'I've noticed you can sometimes change the TV channel when I'm in the middle of watching something. It makes me feel a bit invisible, like I don't really matter to you.'

Example B
'When you change the channel without asking it's so annoying – why do you have to do it all the time? You wouldn't like it if I did it to you – it's rude and disrespectful!'

Which would you prefer to be on the receiving end of? My guess is that you may find A easier to hear . . . B might be a little harder to digest and cause unnecessary friction.

Part #3 Start
This is a great opportunity for the family to think about initiatives they would like specific members, or the whole group, to start. Give everyone a chance to contribute, regardless of how big or small the idea is – and get creative. If you end up with loads of great suggestions that include everyone, you can always get the group to vote on their favourites.

Through the whole exercise, you and your partner may spot some themes that will give you a good insight into how everyone is feeling overall, and you may have been able, reading between the lines, to hear some things that weren't vocalised.

You can both sit down afterwards and talk it through – perhaps you hadn't realised someone was feeling a bit pushed out, or perhaps, through the process, someone was particularly quiet. Maybe you observed you don't sit down together as a family that often, but in doing so you think it would be nice to do a bit more of it. Or maybe there's a challenging dynamic between a couple of the kids that you hadn't noticed before. Based on what you've experienced and subsequently talked through, have a think together if there's a need to have any follow-up conversations, and then decide with your partner about the best way to approach them.

Whatever happens, keep in mind you can use all the information – not just what you hear explicitly, but also what you observe (body language, tone of voice, facial expression etc). All of this is data that will help the whole family develop.

We had a go at the Family MOT exercise. To start with, one of us (not mentioning any names, Ryan) thought it sounded a bit cheesy. But once we got into it, we realised there were loads of things that we hadn't been aware of before, that can now be easily sorted. Plus, the kids – we've each got one from when we were married before – loved it and felt really grown up. It was a nice way to bring everyone together. Would definitely recommend it to others.

Gemma and Ryan, blended couple,
parents and step-parents (32 and 36)

10

Dealing with Crises and Challenges

We can't talk about all the good stuff where blended families are concerned without having a real conversation about what happens when things go wrong, and, most importantly, provide a few ideas about how to handle difficult times.

As we've taken the time to acknowledge, blended families do experience a number of the same challenges as nuclear families. Yet there are a host of unique complexities that a blended family may face, and in this section we'll walk through a number of specific scenarios to help illustrate the points being made. You'll hopefully be able to apply the words and guidance to suit your unique situation. Ready? Let's get into it.

Rupture and repair between parent/child

The health of the relationship between parent and child(ren) can suffer for lots of reasons, which impacts the wider blended family. More often than not these problems are dealt with and resolved fairly easily. Particularly significant ruptures may lead to estrangement, however, especially when the kids are old enough to decide how much contact they want with their parents. Estrangements are more common that you might think, with research indicating that one in five families will deal with some form of it at some point. So how can this be dealt with in the broader blended family context?

There are plenty of circumstances where it might not be particularly healthy for two people to be in contact with one another – for example, where any form of abuse is concerned. However, sometimes ruptures and consequent estrangements occur for less sinister reasons, such as a catalogue of miscommunications, or a lack of ability on one or both sides to resolve smaller incidents healthily and in a timely way. And which, moreover, could have been repaired even more quickly were it not for negative influences and unhelpful mindsets, such as a lack of self-awareness, pride and blame.

In this scenario, to call it an estrangement we are presuming the child is old enough to take responsibility for their own actions, or for the lack of contact to be mutually agreeable, otherwise we would be calling it parental abandonment. While both parent and child have to take responsibility for the healing of their mutual relationship, let's take a look at the role the step-parent could play.

The dynamics here are fairly unique to the blended family. In the case of an estrangement in a nuclear family construct, the other parent is typically highly attached to their child and is unlikely to be supportive of an estrangement. There may also be several friends/family who robustly share their concerns and encourage a repair, putting pressure on the estranged pair to reunite.

By contrast, however, in a blended family the step-parent is often less attached to the child and therefore can make a conscious choice as to what degree they choose to facilitate (or not) the repair of the parent/child relationship. This will inevitably be impacted by the step-parent's personal feelings towards their step-child and/or to what degree they believe the relationship between step-child and their parent has impacted the blended couple relationship negatively. Where a step-parent is asked not to intervene by their partner, or chooses not to, the rupture within the blended family can be fairly substantial, as now one member of the couple is at best neutral towards the idea of a reconciliation, while the other is actively perpetuating it. With no driving force to reunite, the estrangement continues.

Yet, the step-parent is also presumably in a good position to intervene and influence, by virtue of living with their partner. Where the step-parent and step-child have a good relationship, there is the potential for them to step in and encourage progress, be that a conversation or an opportunity to meet, where both parties can begin to work towards a shared understanding and finding a path towards reuniting. The step-parent can, indeed, play a positive role, offering support and empathy, encouraging each to consider their actions and how they feel about them, and by helping to broker contact. The step-parent could also share their own feelings about how the estrangement has impacted them, in order to bring the blended family unit back together. The step-parent may be afforded more permission here to step-in, given they don't have a strong vested interest in seeing a reunion between parent and child – their efforts may be seen as more unbiased.

Where the step-parent and step-child do not have a good relationship, however, it is often tempting for the step-parent to take sides and leap to the defence of their partner. However, this is an opportunity for the step-parent to instead try to see beyond their own difficulties or hurt within the context of their relationship, and encourage their partner to make contact with their child. This may be a difficult path to take, as it may be that the step-parent is even feeling a little relieved their step-child isn't in the picture. Yet it's important to try to see beyond that, in order to recognise that the severing of biological bonds can have a highly detrimental effect on the psyches of both parent and child. Conversely, a step-parent attempting to reunite the parent/child could have a positive impact on the step-parent/ step-child relationship, as the efforts of the step-parent are perceived as kind, helpful and selfless by the step-child.

It's also important to acknowledge first and foremost that the parent themselves may not have the emotional capacity to repair the rupture effectively – which is separate from the desire they may or may not have to have a more positive relationship with their child. The parent ultimately has to shoulder that burden. Yet, if the step-parent also doesn't have the emotional capacity to take a constructive and positive role in helping to improve the relationship between the biological parent and child, either based on their own feelings towards their step-child, or their own woundings, or a combination of both, it's important to try to remain neutral. The parent's decision not to be in contact with their child has to be one they make themselves, entirely free from the negative influence of the step-parent.

In the event of a future reunion, if the step-parent has previously discouraged it behind the scenes, it could well affect the couple dynamic negatively by causing resentment, i.e. *'since the estrangement happened, I now know how much you had been biting your tongue; it's clear you don't actually like my child!'* This could then go on to negatively affect the wider triangular dynamic between the reunited parent and child and step-parent in a variety of different ways.

Where there are significant ruptures, it can often feel hopeless; like things will never change. Regardless of the influence of anyone else, however, the only people that can ultimately choose to focus on building bridges are the estranged pair. If this is you, don't despair, things can change providing you:

- Both actively want to improve things.
- Are willing to look at yourselves and understand the part you've each played in what went wrong.

- Can look at the other side, feel compassion and demonstrate empathy for how they might be feeling.

Having additional children

This is a huge and sensitive subject and hard to cover within the confines of a single chapter, let alone only part of it. A blended family couple may well decide to have additional children together, either in addition to the children you each *both* have, or this may be a first for one of you. Or you may be thinking about adopting a child, if for any reason you aren't able to have (more) biological children.

This has to be a decision for the couple alone, and not one for the children to influence – whatever their age – directly or indirectly. You may be thinking this is an obvious point to make, but although you may not sit your children down and discuss the possibility with them, difficulties can arise if the biological children from one of the previous partnerships make it clear they do not want to have an additional half-sibling. This can be the case for any number of reasons, but is usually down to a fear the child has of being pushed aside, forgotten about or deprioritised.

Naturally this can be the case for nuclear family constructs too. However, feelings of strong attachment to and natural territorial instincts over the parent are generally much more apparent in the case of blended families, as of course the children are unlikely to have the same depth of attachment to the step-parent. So the step-parent can be seen as the one who is the cause of a baby coming onto the scene, taking Mummy/Daddy away from existing children. This can activate the difficult 'drama triangle' situation we looked at in Chapter Eight, where the step-parent takes on the role of attacker, the child (in this scenario) moves into victim position, and the biological parent is set up to rescue.

In reality, this sets up a complex emotional chain reaction in the 'rescuer' parent, particularly if they are the ones to have left the nuclear family home. Feelings of intense guilt can arise, which can be suffocating for them to bear. We looked at guilt in Chapter One, and we can all understand how it develops, yet this is a clear example of how destructive it can be to harbour it for a sustained period of time. In this case, guilty feelings can manifest in a reluctance to not want to 'upset the apple cart' or 'cause' uncomfortable feelings in their children, such as a deeply held fear of abandonment or rejection. For the parent, this moves on to a more practical response, such as a reticence to have children with their step-parent spouse/partner, which in turn creates confusion and resentment, and is a huge problem for the relationship.

If, regardless of the feelings of your children, you don't want to have additional children with your partner, there is nothing wrong with that. BUT – and yes, this is so important it's in capitals – it's vital to name that openly and honestly as soon as you have come to that decision. The longer you leave it, the harder it will be for your partner to respond objectively. However, once armed with the facts, your partner can then choose on their own terms whether or not they are happy to remain in a relationship where the possibility of having biological children of their own, or additional children, is not something the relationship (i.e. *both* parties within it) wants or desires.

The key situation to avoid is one where you would be happy to have more children but have *become* reluctant because your existing children have shared it's not something they want. This dynamic causes immense strain on the couple's relationship. It will be clear that the reason for your indecision, reluctance or avoidance of making concrete plans is down to wanting to appease the children you have, and may well affect the positive regard the step-parent has for their step-children.

If this is an issue you are facing, try to deal with it proactively to avoid damaging your relationship. You could consider professional support to deal with the uncomfortable and perhaps conflicting feelings you are carrying. You can learn to separate them out from your relationship with your partner, and develop tools to appropriately support the child(ren) you already have, as and when you both find out you're expecting.

Experiencing fertility-related loss and grief

Grief is never easy to deal with, and can devastate families. However, fertility-related loss in a blended family can create additional challenges, especially if the children had expressed reluctance for the family to grow further. Key decisions need to be made, such as how to communicate the sad news to the children, assuming the children were aware you and your partner had fallen pregnant.

The baby, had it been born, would have been the half-sibling of any existing children, and therefore the loss may be extremely difficult and sensitive news to share. You'll want to help them make sense of and deal with their feelings, whatever they are. Even if the kids were reluctant to have a half-sibling, news of loss can induce in them a sense of sadness, which is to be expected, but also, and not uncommonly, guilt. They may irrationally wonder: *'has my reluctance to have a half-sibling somehow caused my mum/step-mum to lose the baby?'* This is a lot for a young mind to process, and naturally you will want to reassure them that this was absolutely not the case. Ideally, the couple – both parent and step-parent – would agree *together* the best way to communicate with the child(ren), so both feel their views are heard and understood by the other.

Sharing the news together demonstrates you are a joint team, and role models healthy communication to the kids. It also gives the whole family a chance to talk honestly and openly about how they are coping with the loss, and what it might mean for them. This can then be an opportunity to strengthen the blended family bond, particularly given the topic is so intimate.

Teen/young adult crisis

In any family construct the dreaded teenage years can cause the hair of the most relaxed of characters to turn grey. But what happens when these normal milestones take a more destructive turn, causing harmful habits to form for a temporary or sustained period of time? Yes, these may impact the family dynamic, but of even greater concern are those which pose a threat to the health or physical safety of the young adult(s) in the household.

For negative behaviours limited to the blended family (for example, milder forms of acting out, including shouting or swearing, or behaving passive aggressively, such as refusal to participate in family activities), the blended family couple should agree and align together on how best to deal with this. In some cases the step-parent may well want to take a slight back seat and defer to their partner here – for example, if the couple have only lived together for a relatively short period of time, or if household norms are yet to be fully established. But overall, what happens in the blended family household, and how it's run, is for the adult couple to decide and agree upon.

In Chapter Two we looked at the importance of boundaries, and how to set up behavioural expectations for each individual blended family unit, which may differ slightly from household to household. However, for much more serious 'edge' cases that are household agnostic, it's generally going to be best practice for the co-parenting team to work on a joint strategy to help their child get back to a healthier state of mind. It's important, on both a moral and ethical level, that the co-parents raise their child in a way that aligns with their values, but it is also especially important where the child who is experiencing the life crisis lives between two households (e.g. where Mum and Dad have joint custody). Here are some examples:

- Drug abuse
- Alcohol abuse
- Unhealthy romantic attachments, including abusive behaviours exhibited by your (step-)child's partner
- Anti-social behaviours, such as shoplifting
- Illnesses, such as eating disorders

Without a jointly aligned approach that runs between both houses, both are in danger of being manipulated, with tactics such as lying or splitting (where one is played off against the other), in a bid for the young adult/teenager who is exhibiting the unhealthy behaviours to continue them unchecked. This is not usually done with malicious intent, but it is important to recognise that unless both co-parents are utterly aligned as to the expectations and game plan, there is ample opportunity for their child to act out – which means recovery will be slower.

The step-parent can actually be of great help in these situations. Generally not as emotionally connected as the parent, they're in a strong position to offer support to the family, and specifically their partner. They are also better able to keep a clear(er) head when it comes to plans and strategies being formed to help curb the negative behaviours. They can influence the plans made by the co-parenting team – but, if possible, allowing the co-parents to come up with the right strategy for them here is important.

Instead, the step-parent can move to a position of learning the agreed strategy and doing what they can to reinforce it where appropriate. Their partner, who is one half of the co-parenting team, may find this time incredibly emotionally taxing, and may be taking on additional responsibility to help look after the child who is going through a crisis, and consequently be under a huge amount of strain. So, in addition, the step-parent figure could also step in to keep the rest of their house operating as usual – particularly if other children live there. This may mean taking on a little extra domestic responsibility, taking care of the other kids and so on, until the crisis passes.

Of course, this general rule of thumb isn't going to work for every situation. There will be many households where the second co-parent isn't in the picture, for a variety of reasons, leaving the role of co-parent open to be filled.

In these cases it may well be that the step-parent is called upon to step in, taking on a more traditional hands-on parenting role. Here, it may be more appropriate for the parent to deal with official bodies, such as police/medical teams, with the step-parent operating in the background. Again, during this time, as well as taking on a more proactive role helping to figure out how to tackle the situation, the step-parent can help to reinforce expected behaviours within the home, and take on more of a hands-on parenting role.

Step-parents should avoid taking a protective stance over their partner (the parent) in the household at this stage. Depending on the situation, it's all too easy to do so. If a young adult/teen is behaving destructively, you may well feel incredibly defensive of your partner and (irrationally) want to 'punish' or vent your frustrations at your step-child.

In this case, you are walking a delicate tightrope; as much as you want to support your partner, you may cause additional distress in the household – and this may upset the dynamic and put you in the position of scapegoat later down the line, with, say, partner resentment, step-child anger or protective behaviours from other younger members of the household coming your way.

How you approach your step-child throughout this time will also be a critical juncture in your relationship, and one which could deepen and strengthen your bond over time as they grow older and the crisis passes. Approaching your step-child with patience, empathy and as much understanding as possible will help – but this approach will take up a huge amount of emotional effort and it's likely you will be just as stressed as your partner.

As with any family navigating a crisis, whether short lived or sustained, it can cause a huge amount of stress for the other family members. Consider professional support to help you get through, or at the very least find ways to cope that work for you – going for a run, talking to close friends or journalling are all recognised ways to help people deal with stress.

This may well test the blended family couple dynamic in all sorts of ways. From dealing with the redistribution of domestic labour to increased stress levels to reduced quality time spent together as a couple. Find regular ways to cope that bring you both together as a couple. Making the effort to cook each other dinner or taking the dog for a walk together in the evening a couple of times a week, say, will all pay dividends. And during this time make sure to check-in with one another to:

- Appreciate the efforts your partner is making, and acknowledge how well they're coping, or the impact they're having on helping to resolve things
- Ask if there are things you can do/do less of to help
- Voice what you may need more of/less of

Relationship breakdown

A different type of crisis is one faced by the couple themselves, and this time it's when their relationship breaks down. Where one or both members of the couple are living at least part time with their step-children, it can create a challenging dynamic dominated by unconscious behaviours as each member of the couple strives to cope.

Parents during this time may unconsciously spend a bit more time with their own children, to compensate for a growing rupture and divide in the couple dynamic, and in cases of extreme discord and tension it may be that the children are unwittingly used as pawns. Aligning with their children is an exclusionary tactic, unconsciously designed to help the parent feel safer and stronger in the household dynamic. This can be incredibly hurtful to the step-parent figure.

Step-parents during this time may unconsciously separate a little from their step-children, by projecting their frustrations or hurt towards their partner onto them. Little things they used to find endearing or bite their tongue about suddenly become much bigger bones of contention, which can cause arguments and additional tension. Again, this is an unconscious defensive behaviour, and its purpose may be to begin a withdrawal process designed to help protect the step-parent in the future, if they no longer feel psychologically safe in the blended family household.

What about the kids?

In nuclear families, a threat of parental separation is hard to cope with, considering the splitting that can take place in the child's psyche. For example, the children can assume someone is to blame and wonder who that might be – and if they have formed a stronger attachment with the parent they perceive to be 'at fault', then this can have a negative impact on their sense of self – for example, a rejection of the aspects of themselves they once perceived to be similar to the parent who is 'in the wrong'.

Children within blended family households don't feel this sense of divided loyalties or splitting in the same way. Instead, they tend to naturally 'side' with their parent – and this can be especially pronounced when each member of the couple has brought children to live together under one roof. This can happen whether a threat of separation is made explicit, or simply in the case of prolonged periods of unrest and tension between the couple, potentially manifesting overtly with withdrawal from the step-parent or an active defense of their parent.

Children in blended families are also acutely aware of what happens when parents separate, having been through it once before when their own did just that. This can leave them with a sense of hyper-vigilance, and heightened intuition, which can render even the most concerted efforts of the blended family couple useless, as the children pick up on the merest hint of tension, and naturally assume a split is imminent – even when it isn't. All of this can cause a feeling of unease, additional stress, worry or concern.

None of the behavioural dynamics described above are conducive to a healthy household, and so it's key the blended family couple sit down privately and talk properly about what's going on, for the benefit of themselves, their relationship and the household.

Some things to consider:

- What's your intention – do you and your partner wish to work through the crisis, or begin a process of separation?
- Once the decision has been made, how can you both move forward with your decision – what do you both need?

241

- What are your thoughts on how to improve household dynamics in the short term? Is there anything that needs immediate attention that you need to discuss jointly?

Couple separation

Separating blended family couples will go through similar stages to any separating couple – the decision making process, the ensuing grief cycle, practical considerations such as living arrangements, and then perhaps divorce, if you are married. It's not a linear step-by-step process, and many of the stages overlap. However, as usual, there are some specific situations that only a blended family will need to consider, as separation can create all sorts of emotional setbacks for each member of the group.

- The parent may feel they are losing their team mate, the one who they built a blended family with, who helped them to make sense of and recover from their separation or divorce from the children's mum or dad. Or they may feel hopeless – another relationship ending, what's wrong with me?
- The step-parent may feel similarly, and additionally may be aware of a sense of isolation or being cut adrift from the blended family unit they have been a part of, suddenly excluded from their step-children's lives. Blended family separations can be fairly blunt and swift, without enough attention given to the process of ending, to honour the relationship between step-child/step-parent.
- The children may feel a sense of loyalty towards their parent, but also a sense of guilt or sadness towards the step-parent they

may have bonded with, and disappointment that the relationship is ending.

Additionally, if both members of the couple have brought children
into the equation, and for some time you've all been living under
the same roof, a separation is likely to mean the children will need
to divide and go back to living only with their parent (or between
co-parents, if a joint custody arrangement is in place). This could cause
a period of unrest and destabilisation in the children, quite easily
generating feelings of confusion, grief and sadness among them, as
well as anger and frustration – either directed at the adults, or each
other, as a way to express their feelings.

In these instances, do take plenty of time to agree as a couple how
to handle next steps. Getting your own heads clear, and developing a
joint plan, while taxing, will help to smooth along the conversations
with your children/step-children.

Then, sit down together and explain to all of the children what's
happening. You'll want to adjust your explanations and narrative to
suit the youngest member of the group, no doubt, but in these cases,
and where much older children or young adults are concerned, you
can make time to sit down with them separately and answer questions
they may have that aren't suitable for the younger ones.

It's important to avoid telling your children without the step-
parent there. While they don't have biological/legal ties to your
children, they may have been a part of their lives for many years,
and a step-parent is an important role that will have influenced your
children one way or another. The feelings of love and commitment
to your children that your partner developed as a result of your
relationship with them are real, and it is important to honour
them, for all your sakes. Here, the kids will see they are important
to their step-parent, which will reinforce their sense of self. It also

demonstrates that relationship endings are just as important as their beginnings, and handling them with great care and respect will pay off in the future, with regards how your children conduct their own relationships.

Finally, it gives you a chance to work together as a team and be there to answer any questions the children may have. Having an aligned and joint narrative is important for stability, and avoids giving the children a sense of adult complexities, such as hidden agendas and manipulation, before they are old enough to process them properly.

As with all separations, it's common for the desire to separate/ divorce to be one-sided – or at least one person may want it more than the other. However, if one half of the couple is reluctant to accept the separation, a period of living in limbo can ensue, and the household can't move forward until both members of the adult couple are aligned. Living in limbo is really hard for lots of reasons:

- You tread on eggshells around each other – not wishing to cause further distress to someone already in emotional pain, or not wanting to give the partner who has instigated the separation any more cause to want to do so.
- You misinterpret signals, and fantasise a reunion is imminent.
- Resentful feelings start to build up, i.e.'*why won't my partner change their mind, can't they see we're much better together?*' Or '*why can't my partner just accept I don't want to be with them anymore?*'

With big life changes such as separations, it takes time before our hearts and emotional brains can accept the new situation, and allow our rational heads to move in and help us move on. However, none of the dynamics described above are conducive to moving on – they keep us stuck in the past. They create distress, cause decline in the mental health of the individuals in the family, and affect the group dynamic. So, as painful as it might be, it's important to take steps to move forward. Living in limbo is incredibly hard, and keeping up a pretence or living in hope of a reunion with your partner is not good for your mental health. So, once the decision is made, ensure everyone in the household is aware as soon as you've agreed next steps together.

> I had been with my partner for many years, and had built a great relationship with my step-son. When we separated, my ex found it hard to accept at first, and financial circumstances also meant we were living in the house together for a while after too. Perhaps thinking we would reconcile, he refused to let us break the news to my step-son – and given he wasn't my child I didn't feel I could override him on it. So, I had to pretend for months when he was staying in the house with us, which was really hard. When he was finally told, my ex insisted on doing it alone, which caused a lot of hurt and anger on my part. Then to make matters worse, my step-son regrettably overheard one of the rows we had about it – it wasn't my step-son's fault we were separating and my outburst must have hurt him.
>
> What advice would I give to other blended families separating? Well, I would say do your best to keep your conversations about such sensitive topics well out of earshot of the kids. My circumstances made this hard for me, but it's definitely something I would guard against in the future. I also don't think you should live under the same roof for a moment longer than is strictly necessary; it makes the dynamic much

harder than it needs to be. Finally, I would say the kids should be told by both their parent and step-parent together. In my case so many years had been put into building the family and the various relationships, it felt wrong to keep it a secret and not be there to tell him.

Lara, step-mother (42)

The dos and don'ts of separation:

DO

- Sit down with your partner and agree how you want to handle arrangements as far as the children are concerned.
- Agree on what you feel is fair and equitable for all of the kids involved, to avoid unnecessary feelings of rejection or a sense that one sibling over another is 'the favourite'.
- Tell the children in a timely way so you can all begin the process of moving forward.

DON'T

- Tell your children separately. Ensure you tell them together, as a team, and consider an age appropriate way to do this.
- Unless there are very good or unavoidable reasons, don't create separate narratives that are confusing and upsetting for the children, and disrespectful to your partner.
- Feel like you need to do this alone. Couples therapists are there to see you through relationship endings, not just mid-relationship crises. Sitting down with someone qualified and impartial to formulate your plan is a good idea, both to help

you process and come up with the right practical solutions for your family.

Post separation

The couple also need to consider how the relationship with their respective step-children will change once the separation occurs. This can be very difficult, particularly if the bond is close and was forged over a number of years. It's an odd feeling and is unlike separation between nuclear families, because in these cases, you won't have a legal obligation to provide financially for your step-children, and you won't have any automatic rights in relation to custody or visitation, unless you have adopted them.

When nuclear families separate, although day-to-day practicalities generally change – living arrangements and so on – the *relational ties* between parent and child remain intact. Couples rightly go to great lengths to preserve these ties through custody arrangements, and reassuring statements such as 'I'll always be your mummy/daddy, we will always love you and that will never change'.

Because familial ties are different, and legalities are seen as less complex, blended family separations can often be swifter than nuclear separations, and this can cause a great amount of hurt for all concerned. Particularly in cases where the step-parent has been a part of the child or children's lives for many years, it is highly probable that close bonds have developed and, in fact, there may be a great desire on both parts for the relationship to be preserved and to survive any separation between parent/step-parent.

It's important for both members of the couple to align, attempting to understand each other's point of view. Some questions to ask yourselves and each other are:

- What kind of relationship would you like with your step-children post-separation?
- What kind of relationship would you like your partner to have with their step-children post-separation?
- What would the children like to happen? What is in their best interests?
- Do you want and are you prepared for that relationship to change over time – for example, what happens when either of you meets someone new? This is especially important as this may make it inappropriate for contact to continue, as the outgoing step-parent will naturally not be a part of the new blended family group (and, in fact, may in the future be pre-oc-cupied with creating a new one themselves). In these cases the step-child may well feel torn and not know how to honour their parent's new relationship, while at the same time trying to maintain a relationship with the outgoing step-parent. The step-child may also feel jealous if their outgoing step-parent meets a person who has children, who may well become the outgoing step-parent's priority.

If the intention is to have a relationship with your step-children post separation, consider the following when communicating with them:

- Do express your love and care for them.
- Allow them to share what relationship they would like to have with you.
- If you can, make it clear that you will be there for them if they need you.
- Depending on their age, you may also wish to share that the nature of your relationship will naturally change and evolve

when either you or their mum/dad meets someone new. It's important to normalise that; kids often can't anticipate the broader and longer term impact of situations occurring in the present – as an older authority figure, you can help with that.

Bereavement

Grieving journeys are unique to everyone, and personal loss is never easy. The level of grief we experience can vary greatly depending on the nature of the relationships we have, but what can be a particularly interesting phenomenon for our blended families is the expectations of those around us, and our own reactions to dealing with death within the context of these family groups. Let's break it down:

Death of a step-child

Few would argue the fact that the premature death of a child is an utter tragedy. The feelings of disbelief, unjustness and unfairness that someone has passed away before their time, and the guilt that can leave us feeling – as though we'd like to be able to take their place – are completely normal. Thankfully this is a rarity. However, when the worst happens, for our blended family, the grief may be heightened by an unforeseen force. We would expect the death of a child to be life altering for any parent, and indeed we know that, for those that it happens to, life is reported never to be the same again.

Yet family systems can unwittingly take out their frustration and anger (a natural part of the grieving process) on the step-parent, who can feel relegated to the periphery. They can be made to feel their grieving process is immaterial – or at least secondary compared to that of the parents; little more than something that should be minimised to create space for the ones with unspoken permission to grieve.

If you are in this position as a step-parent, you will know that in developing a strong bond with your step-child during their lifetime, perhaps caring for them as if they were your own, your grief is real, and at times it may feel as if you can't carry on. Know that you are entitled to it. It is not something that can be rationed or measured in the absence of being your step-child's biological or adopted parent.

I cared for my husband's children throughout their formative years and into their adulthood. They called me Mum. I was the only mother figure in their lives, after their biological mother was unable to care for them as a result of chronic mental health issues. It was only after I separated from my husband that my step-son, Jake, developed a terminal illness, and subsequently passed away when he was only twenty-four. I had been in regular contact with him and had spent time caring for him as his illness progressed. His father, meanwhile, had since remarried and moved abroad. When Jake died, my grief was extensive, and I suffered tremendously. Yet, the narrative and expectations of those around me were to concentrate well wishes on the biological parents, and the new step-parent figure (who had had little to do with her adult step-children in the short time she had been married to my ex-husband). I felt as if my grief had been silenced, and as if it wasn't acceptable to my family, who left me to deal with my grief alone. Unsurprisingly this deeply impacted me; I felt utterly unsupported by those around me.

Jill, step-mother and mother (52)

If you find yourself in a similar situation, speak up if you can, and try to share how you're feeling with trusted friends and members of the family you feel safe with. Find a therapist. Despite it being in the twenty-first century, the world is still on a journey to understand and make room for these sorts of relationships. Collectively, we will get there, but in the meantime your responsibility is to yourself. Do what you need to do in the dynamic to acknowledge and attend to your own grieving process, and focus on honouring the bond you had with your step-child. From a spiritual perspective, how wonderful that your life path was able to converge with your step-child's, even for a short time. The time you did have together was an opportunity to learn and grow, and you can cherish the memories you have of them.

Death of a step-parent

I have heard many experiences over the years of step-children who have lost beloved step-parents in their adulthood. Again, the grieving process is agnostic of title, and the heart simply recognises what *is*, rather than how we tell ourselves we *should* feel. As we know, the bond between step-parent and step-child can be unshakeable, and something that can take on a flavour unique to that of the parent-child relationship. It isn't necessarily worse or better – but it is certainly different. And so it is not uncommon for the grieving process here to be long and arduous.

The interesting pattern that can emerge for our blended families in this specific scenario, however, is the idea that grief can somehow be assuaged with the knowledge there are 'extra parent figures' around – and their presence can almost make up for the death of one of them.

When my step-dad passed away, I was devastated. I was only in my twenties, and Rob had been in my life since I was five years old. I am close to my parents too, yet both my step-parents had become incredibly important figures in my life. In the early months after his death, and I guess trying to make me feel better, several of my friends commented that, while Rob dying was sad, at least I still had the other three parents, and at least my 'real' mum and dad were still alive. I know they were trying to help, but to me it just came across as really insensitive, and it didn't mirror my experience at all. From then on I tried to keep my grief hidden from them.

Olivia, bereaved step-daughter (27)

We must recognise, however, that we are not always close to our step-parent figures – in the same way we are not always close to our parents. If you find yourself in Olivia's position but you simply don't connect with her level of devastation, it's important to allow whatever feelings you do have to exist without judgement. Mourning someone's death by honouring the impact they did have on your life is perfectly possible without feeling knocked for six by their passing. Remember that your process is yours alone – it doesn't need justifying.

We tend to romanticise people in death, and while there is no issue with that, if that isn't how you feel then that's perfectly okay. Some adult step-children, in their most private moments, express a sense of relief that their step-parent has died. Many adult children do too, when an abusive or estranged parent dies. If someone causes you significant harm in life, how on earth can you be *expected* to mourn their death?

We all have the capacity to feel the full range of human emotion; this is important in order to be healthy. The only expectation you should have of yourself is congruence – so, in private, if you feel happy, relieved, grateful that someone is no longer around, then allow it. If we have learned anything from our blended family exploration, it is that we need to be true to ourselves. For so many reasons people will judge unhelpfully from the sidelines, but in the end none of it matters. Just tune in to what you're feeling, and don't try to change them.

11

Bringing It All Together

We've covered a lot of ground so far, but you may only have a few minutes, and those that have been with me since Chapter One may feel the need for a refresher. So, below you'll find a snapshot of the whole book. Grab a cuppa and settle in!

One
Understanding Grownups

- Parents: Those recently separated may be carrying a lot of guilt or anger. Find ways to deal with this, so you don't develop an overcompensating attitude towards your children or a placating/bitter attitude towards your ex. Consciously consider custody arrangements that work for everyone involved; resist defaulting to the status quo to conform with unconscious societal expectations.
- Step-parents: Your role can be seen through a challenging (read: negative) cultural and societal lens. Learn where this comes from, and appraise your own circumstances on their own merit. Do what you can to take responsibility for what's going on for you, don't let unhelpful stereotypes get you down.

- Words and titles matter. When it comes to addressing step-parents, however, forcing false intimacy will create barriers. The kids may choose to apply their own special nicknames or titles to the step-parent – but only on their terms. Until then, start with first names.

Two
Understanding Kids

- Tiny ones (0–5) – particular sensitivity is needed to balance the input of the co-parenting team with the roles and responsibilities of the step-parent. The blended couple should align regularly on the division of childcare. Where custody is shared between households, co-parents should align as far as possible on daily routines and habits, helping to stabilise and provide consistency for the kids.
- Little ones (6–12) – this age range can arguably be the easiest to transition from nuclear to blended family. Childcare gradually becomes less hands-on, there is enough neuro-plasticity in young brains to help the kids adjust and accept 'the new normal' relatively quickly, and the stress/big changes that teens experience are still a few years away.
- Teens (13–18) – teens are challenging in any environment, including nuclear families. Avoid getting caught up in their big emotional swings; the more you can be both a consistent and positive presence, the more quickly trust will build. Step-parents, if you are new to parenting, tap into the many resources that already exist to understand your teen step-children a little better.
- Adult children (18+) – parents play a critical role in setting the

tone, to ensure their children feel considered and safe as the family evolves, and to protect the step-parent from unnecessary attacks. Parents can also role model clear boundaries and respectful behaviour towards other adults in the broader dynamic, such as their ex-partner. Adult children nonetheless should take responsibility for their own approach to the blended family, contributing to it as consciously and healthily as possible. While perhaps hard, open communication ensures important things aren't left unsaid – but listen up, parents: this is only going to be possible, if you, as the older authority figures, create a safe enough environment for this to happen. The step-parent should encourage relationships between parent and child(ren). Even though a hands-on parenting role won't be needed with this age group, step-parents can work towards being a positive and supportive influence, fostering respect and trust over time.

Three
Understanding the Couple

- Meeting someone new after a long term relationship ends can be joyful. The blended couple often have more 'adult' time than their nuclear counterparts, as custody arrangements are generally shared. This provides greater opportunity for the couple to focus on the health of their relationship, and keep things fresh.
- Don't rush it. Before the kids are introduced, this is an opportunity, in addition to having fun and enjoying each other, to work through the implications of introducing kids to the dynamic. Discuss your hopes and fears, and how you plan to

work together to support the kids' healthy development, as well as your own mental health and that of the relationship.

- Once the children are introduced, even if it's not the case you naturally have more adult time (e.g. for those with full time custody arrangements) ensure you make time for it. You will need it to deal with the emotional and practical complexity that comes with this terrain. Protecting the quality of the relationship will also help you to be an even more effective parent/step-parenting team, which is the crucial ingredient of a successful blended family.

Four
Making Introductions

- When meeting prospective step-children, remember that their response to meeting you isn't personal, it's about what you may represent to them.
- Clothing choices – this may seem trivial but a) we know that first impressions count and b) your choice of outfit will signal a lot about you, and will be influenced by the type of activity you choose to all do together, as well as the children's ages. Think about how you want to portray yourself and go from there.
- Choice of activity – this can cause concern for our blended couples. This chapter details some options for different age groups, but the key is to consciously create a safe, comfortable and lighthearted environment. Focusing on a specific activity provides common ground and something to bond over, distracting from heavier subjects that are too serious for now.
- Adult behaviours – if you focus on only three qualities, make

them kindness, patience and calm. These are good foundations for most relationships, but for step-relationships in particular, psychological safety is critical from the start. You will have plenty of chances to reveal the rest of your personality over the coming months.

- Child behaviours – kids may respond to meeting Mum or Dad's new partner in unexpected or challenging ways, which is why the golden trio of calm, patience and kindness are so critical. If the step-parent is on the receiving end of attacks or rudeness, defer to the parent for admonishments or broader expectation setting, but don't be afraid to gently set some boundaries here. This demonstrates self-worth and role models good behaviours the kids can learn from.

- Work together ahead of the meeting to align on the narrative that's age appropriate, in anticipation of tricky questions. Let the parent handle anything unforeseen.

- When introducing two sets of children, talk through in advance any potential areas of difference in your respective parenting style relating to the activities you've chosen to do, thereby creating a relaxed and consistent atmosphere on the day itself (e.g. whether or not to have pudding after lunch). Children in blended families have a heightened vigilance around fairness, and having the same approach as one another will help lay the groundwork for healthy step-sibling relationships from the start.

- Now is the time when people question whether the incoming step-parent should meet the ex-partner. This is not a prerequisite. Blended families need time to come together in their own right, and it can take children much longer to adjust if 'old' and 'new' adult relationships are visibly combined from the start. This dynamic can also be incredibly emotionally taxing. If it's right in your circumstance, then go for it. But if just one of you feels uncomfortable, do not force it.

- Make an exception for significant upcoming milestones relating to the children (e.g. a wedding), however. Meeting your partner's ex/your ex's new partner for the first time at an already emotionally charged occasion is not for the faint hearted. Meeting earlier ahead of time has lots of benefits, including breaking the ice. Ensure any meetings feel psychologically safe by considering the time of day, location etc.

Five
What Happens When Things Get Serious: First Steps

Staying over:

- Where no kids are involved, this often happens early on, but take time to plan when the right time might be in your circumstances.
- The age of the children, how long you've been together and the dynamics so far will tell you whether you want to start off in separate rooms, or skip straight to staying in the same bed.
- Do explain to the kids that your partner is going to be staying over, sharing context if appropriate to build understanding.
- On the night, go low key or make it a fun event the kids can get excited about. Creating positive associations with these events can help at this early stage.
- Sleeping in the same bed: Don't be afraid to take your time with this one – for younger kids, having a relative stranger sleeping in Mummy or Daddy's bed is not insignificant. If

they're used to coming into their parent's room during the night, this habit will be disrupted by the presence of someone else in the room.

Holidays:

- Holidays are great fun for our burgeoning blended families. But only take this step if the kids have forged a good enough bond in the time they've spent with your partner to withstand living in close proximity for a sustained period of time.
- If you can, involve the kids in deciding where to go.
- If you both have kids, invite them all. (Though I appreciate that, for young adults at uni, a family holiday might not be that appealing!) Don't separate anyone out, especially in these early stages, as favouritism woundings leave understandably deep scars for step-children with step- or half-siblings.
- Make time to talk through finer elements that are unique to the blended family. Sleeping arrangements while on holiday, contact with the co-parent who's left at home, ensuring everyone has enough personal space etc . . . all of these things deserve consideration.

Moving in:

- Moving in together is a big deal – for the incomer, the one who's household is about to have someone else move in and the kids. Take the time to understand your own needs, what's truly important, what are the 'nice to haves' . . .
- Proactively share any worries or concerns. As with any

relationship, compromise will be needed, but do take the time to listen, and then try to meet each other's needs. What is really a big deal vs something you can tolerate – especially if it makes your partner happy.

- Talk to everyone in the household about it and allay any concerns the kids have.
- Parents: You may need to start to 'broker' a little more now the relationship has got to this stage. You're likely wearing the triple hat of parent, partner and peacekeeper. As the lynchpin between your partner and your kids, while it's important they forge their own relationships, you can help by being sensitive to the needs of each.

Having another baby:

- Pregnancy and parenting best practice may have changed since one or both of you last went through this process. It's okay to repeat some things that worked really well last time, but also find your own way of parenting together.
- Having overwhelming feelings of love and affection for your biological child that may well outweigh your feelings for your step-children is normal: don't beat yourself up.
- However, do treat all the children as a group of siblings, part of the same blended family, with the same rules, opportunities and outward displays of affection for each.
- While your bonds will be different with each, make every effort to include all the children in helping to welcome a new baby to the household. Give siblings opportunities to bond, which may mean they spend more time in your household at first.

Engagement:

- Share the news with your co-parent before the kids do. This shows respect, and gives them a chance to prepare – they may be on the receiving end of questions or comments that need sensitive handling.
- If you and your partner each have children, tell them all together.
- Create space for the kids to express how they're feeling. It's not your job to 'fix' everything, and time is a great healer when it comes to adjusting to sensitive news. However, like grown-ups, kids generally feel safer if they know it's okay to show their sadness or share their worries. Plus, if you do discover any obvious ways to help them adjust, you can always take steps to meet those needs.
- Mark the occasion in a meaningful way for all of you. Reinforcing the concept of the new family team will help to establish and integrate everyone.

Weddings:

- Involve the kids in the planning, but only where you are genuinely happy to have input. Whether you're getting married for the first time or not, weddings are deeply personal and you deserve to put your own stamp on yours.
- Do make an effort to allocate the kids roles. Don't force them to do anything they're uncomfortable with, of course, but showing you'd like them to be a part of it will reinforce their sense of belonging and inclusion – vital aspects of psychological safety in our blended families.
- On the day itself, keep speech content sensitive to young ears

who may, despite being really happy for you both, feel a bit disloyal to Mum/Dad at home.

- Plan a family trip post-wedding, in addition to the more traditional honeymoon. I call this the Family Moon! It can be as lavish or as frugal as your budget allows; it's not about spending money you don't have, it's about celebrating your new family together.

Six
Handling Conflict

- Conflict is inevitable, especially in families, and certainly within blended families where lots of different personality styles converge. When expressed and dealt with healthily, conflict generally means opportunity rather than a red flag – to communicate our needs, tolerate differences, and to live more harmoniously together.
- Our relationship with conflict is connected to our relationship with authority, i.e. our approach to conflict is informed by the example our caregivers modelled.
- So, we have a big responsibility to look at how we handle conflict as adults – and it's even more important with children/step-children in the mix. By role modelling how to handle conflict healthily, we avoid 'handing down' our struggles to the next generation.
- We generally handle conflict badly when we are fearful of another's response, as it activates our 'fight or flight' instincts. We generally either come out fighting by raising our voice and saying things we don't mean, or we withdraw completely. Neither are positive for our blended families!

- The older the children are, the more they (like the adults) will bring their own personal set of behavioural norms, values and beliefs. All of these differences need a little time to air before the blended family can settle and start to harmonise.
- The three basics you need in your toolkit to help you resolve conflict in your blended household more quickly are:

  1. A growth mindset
  2. Be brave
  3. Get conscious

- In general, when trying to resolve conflict with step-children, consider these three golden rules:

  1. Take your authority seriously. Take the time to think about how to position what you have to say, where and when you plan to raise the topic.
  2. Role model healthy communication. Actively listen and don't jump in if the kids find the conversation hard. Whether they are kids or teens, they're still learning the ropes. In return, share your concerns clearly, alongside the behaviour/action that is causing tension – and what you would like or expect to change.
  3. Keep it up. The more you approach differences in this way, the more this style of healthier communication will become 'the norm' in your blended household. It will get easier over time.

Seven
The Blended Family in its Early Stages

- Every member of the blended family will bring their own preferred routines, expectations, structures and traditions picked up from their own childhoods or previous family dynamics. Don't feel you need to blindly rinse and repeat. Taking the time to establish rituals and norms that work for your household is one of the nicest aspects of the process of establishing your own blended family.

- Adults need a good level of self-awareness to understand their own needs, voice them, and work together to get them met.

- One of the most rewarding things about learning to understand, value and then voice your own needs is that, in doing so, you'll be teaching the kids in the household to be aware of theirs too. The therapist in me would love this to be taught in schools – so many problems in adulthood seem to stem from people not understanding what their own needs are, and even when they do, they may not have the courage to share them appropriately with those closest to them. Learning this from an early age will pay dividends later on.

- Learning to understand and place value on your own needs doesn't mean getting your way all the time. *Compromise* is essential in our blended family, especially in the early stages where relationships are newer and bonds are fragile.

- A little negotiation and prioritisation of the time/energy/resources/needs you each have will help both the family and the individuals within it grow.

- Balancing everyone's needs depends on many factors, e.g. the consequences of each, and how much they mean to everyone involved. If decisions typically settle in one person's favour, take steps to rebalance the power dynamic.

- Pay attention to the nuances and needs of each relationship within the blended family, and invest in each one appropriately. For example, step-parents will play a variation of the role in relation to their step-child according to things like their respective age and gender identity, the level of desire each has to bond with the other, and the presence of the co-parent, among other things. The emphasis placed on the roles of caregiver vs role-model vs mentor vs emotional or practical supporter will change accordingly.

Eight
How the Family Evolves

- Our experience of groups in our adulthood – whether we feel they are safe or unsafe, exciting or dangerous, comfortable or uncomfortable – is based on our experience of groups in our formative years.
- We each carry a life script – a behavioural template based on past experience. This informs our perception of our families, and the role we play within them. By becoming aware of your own, you can start to challenge your perception of, and behaviour towards, your blended family.
- There are several different types of roles people fall into when part of a group. Some common ones include the 'victim', the 'aggressor', the 'rescuer', as well as different states of mind – such as 'parent', 'adult' or 'child'. It's important to understand what might be going on in your family on an unconscious level,

to make it easier to spot and deal with any unhelpful patterns.

- Over time, to reduce fatigue and a build up of resentment, you can learn to only step into these roles appropriately and consciously.
- Allocating practical roles – key considerations:
  - o Household tasks can take on particular significance in a blended family, based on prior associations from previous family dynamics. People may expect to take on responsibility X, say, or resent the idea of taking on responsibility Y, simply because this was how it was *previously*. For more traditional family set-ups, tasks may not have been divided fairly, or with the full consent/willingness of the person expected to do them (for example, in forms of controlling relationships, or relationships conforming to traditional gender roles).
  - o The blended couple should discuss *together* how they ideally want domestic labour to be allocated. Trying something new, saying 'no', or expressing your preferred way of doing things can feel incredibly empowering and reparative.
  - o Half- and step-sibling dynamics can be challenged too, in cases where parental expectations between each set of children are inconsistent. Resentment, frustration and envy will grow where kids feel rules are different per person. For the health of the family, the blended couple should develop a consistent approach – and not be afraid to reinforce it – until everyone gets into a routine.
- Share out responsibilities to all, based on preference and capability level. In a blended family, ensuring each member is contributing, feels valued and useful, will build an important sense of belonging and community.

Nine
Strengthening Your Blended Family

- Create rituals once the family has established. This helps to define the family identity and promotes a deeper sense of belonging – the basis for meaningful psychological growth.
- Blended families have an opportunity to define their values. This allows everyone to feel part of the team, imbuing a sense of pride and purpose, which is vital for long-term motivation and satisfaction.
- Where bad habits have started to creep in, a clear set of family values can help to reset the dynamic, and allow people to talk through and overcome any differences.
- The blended family can also come together and stand for something by defining their family motto. This fosters pride and a shared understanding.
- Once the family is established, and in a clear routine where people know what's expected of them, and know they belong, they feel safe, all of which allows our families to thrive, and our family members to flourish.

Ten
Dealing with Crises and Challenges

Some of the topics in this chapter in particular are incredibly sensitive, and I would recommend you read it in full to truly appreciate some of the unique considerations that the blended family can face in these situations. However, I've attempted to summarise one or two key points from each of the topics we covered below.

Having additional children:

- The decision to have more kids is complex and is something existing children may attempt to weigh in heavily on. However, this is a decision for the blended couple alone to make. Plenty of children, even in nuclear family set-ups, resent the idea of having siblings. But they usually come around once they realise there will be no less love coming their way as a result – this is no different for blended families. Work together to help the broader family unit deal with any difficult feelings around this, prioritising reassurance and support.

Experiencing fertility-related loss and grief:

- It's important to share the news with existing children together, if you experience any sort of fertility-related loss that existing children may be aware of. Particularly so in dynamics where there was initial resistance to the idea of gaining a half-sibling; feelings can be incredibly intense, as children may irrationally blame themselves for the loss. Open and sensitive handling of this topic can be healing for everyone and help to bring the blended family together.

Rupture between parent/child:

- Step-parents: regardless of your personal views, if you can't play a positive role in encouraging reparations, take care to hold a neutral position when it comes to strained or estranged relationships between your partner and their child (regardless of their age). The bond between parent and child is deep and complex, and should generally be encouraged (despite how you may feel towards your step-child).

- Parents: take active steps to open up communication channels with your child, however hard it might be. If part of the disagreement(s) involve your partner, don't prioritise one relationship over another, or let that get in the way. Attempt to work towards the relationship you would like to have with each separately. Even if your child is an adult, you are still their parent and, as such, are a key authority figure and it is appropriate you make a move to try to resolve things. If your child refuses contact, then, assuming they are an adult, it may be difficult to hear – but it is their prerogative. In this case, seek support from your partner, respect your child's decision, and in the future, when things have settled, they may well reach out to rekindle things, so don't lose hope.

Teen/young adult crisis:

- Teens generally go through a stage of atypical behaviour as a result of a growing independence plus intense hormonal and physical changes. We have all been there! For minor cases that affect the blended household, the blended couple can work together to deal with it – for example, giving appropriate space, setting boundaries and providing clear expectations.
- Don't forget about the needs of the couple – and of you both as individuals – during this time . . . You will need all the strength you can get to deal with the testing domestic dynamic.
- For more serious cases, featuring severe acting out, e.g. dangerous/anti-social behaviours, the co-parenting team should ideally come together to form an aligned cross-household approach. Together, they can create a consistent set of

boundaries, and manage any external agencies, e.g. medical teams that are involved.

- This can be a really hard time for all concerned; as well as looking after their own needs, step-parents may need to step forward and take more responsibility for looking after things at home, allowing the co-parenting team to focus on their teen.

Blended couple relationship breakdown:

- The couple should work together on the best way to manage things in the short term, working through what they each want as an outcome for their relationship as quickly as possible. This will enable them to maintain the household dynamic, look after themselves, and begin to take positive steps towards dealing with their decision.

Blended couple separation:

- Difficult emotions and feelings will surface (guilt, loneliness, sadness, anger etc). Take care of yourself, so you can both come together to look after the kids' emotional needs. Try couples therapy to communicate and process jointly, individual therapy, and talking to respective friends and family to process alone, and keep an eye on physiological needs such as sleep, diet and exercise.
- Tell the kids together – particularly if you have both been a couple for a long time and the children are close to their step-parent:
  o They don't need to know all the details.
  o Reassure them this was a grown-up decision that wasn't made because of them.

272

o Remind them they are safe.
o Make them aware of any practical impact on them personally, e.g. a house move.

Post separation:

• One of the biggest topics that separates blended families from other family types is that step-parents don't typically have custody rights (adoption of step-child notwithstanding). Consider the level of contact you want post-separation, including how things might change as and when you move on, and communicate sensitively to the kids.

Bereavement – death of a child:

• Family systems can find it hard to recognise the grief of a step-parent – particularly so if the blended couple have separated beforehand. Yet step-parents may have played a primary parenting role over a long period of time. Therefore, losing step-children is a tragedy that can have a profound impact on step-parents, as well as other parents. Don't force the grieving process, as it will be unique to you and the relationship you shared. Do take the time to seek solace and support from those that know you best.

Bereavement – death of a step-parent:

• The type and depth of your response to your step-parent's death will be unique to you and there are no rights or wrongs.
• There is nothing wrong if you don't grieve extensively for someone you weren't particularly close to in life, particularly if

you feel they caused you harm. If this is you, don't beat yourself up – grieving brings up lots of unexpected feelings, which settle over time.

- However, those who had a strong relationship with their stepparent may feel devastated by their death, sometimes akin to losing a parent. If this is you, be prepared for some 'helpful' comments from those close to you, who may point out that by virtue of being part of a blended family you are, in fact, lucky to have several parents 'left'. Take the time to honour the opportunity you had to learn from someone who was brought into your life for the time they were here.

This is only the start of the conversation

So, reader, now we're at the end, what would I ideally like you to take away, above all else? Successful blended families are greater than the sum of their parts; for them to work, everyone has to pull their weight – and for them to flourish, every member of one has to work through their own challenging experiences.

We know that taking responsibility for what is yours to own can often be a tricky undertaking. Take on too much and it can be exhausting for you, and enable others to behave badly. Take on too little, however, and it forces other people to deal with your own woundings/pain/negative attitude – delete as appropriate.

Yet it's worth taking the time to figure out and own your part, as blended families can be joyful and incredibly rewarding. But, like all the best things in life, they take work to make them work. Plus, they *are* often misunderstood, they are still less common than other family structures (for now), they *are* more complex than some other types of family group, they do face unique challenges, and they *are* often unhelpfully 'othered' by society. Which is precisely why they deserve extra advocacy, support, love and attention.

I am passionate about blended families and proud of the ones I am a part of. I hope *Step Up* has given you a fresh perspective and encouraged you to be passionate, invest in and be proud of yours too – it's certainly a conversation that deserves a lot more air time in order to truly do it justice.

Acknowledgements

To everyone at Headline who were part of bringing *Step Up* to life, some of whom I've met but many more I know have been a part of it behind the scenes. Special thanks to Zoe Blanc who found me in the first place and got in touch to see if I'd be interested in writing a book, and then helped to get the commission over the line. To Anna Steadman, who edited the text and steered throughout, Anna Herve, who copyedited the text, Nikki Sinclair, who did the first proofread, and Kathy Callesen, who cast an eagle eye over the final version. To the typesetter, the publicity, marketing and production teams and to everyone else I don't know but am grateful to from afar. This has been a fantastic experience, and I am so thankful for your wise and invaluable insights throughout the project.

To everyone in the step/blended families I've been a part of over the years. You've all taught me so much, one way or another, and I'm grateful for all of it. None of us can say we haven't made one or two mistakes along the way, but there has been plenty of fun and lots of love to balance them out!

To A, and the minis, I am so happy we are part of each other's lives and so grateful for the step-family we've worked hard to nurture, and from which we all get so much joy.

A, as you know, one of the many things that we both bonded over was the fact we both had tremendous role models in our respective step-fathers over the years, and so a special thank you to both of them for enriching our lives.

Finally, A, you have formed the most brilliant co-parenting team with H, and I want you both to know I very much admire and respect how you handle everything, from afar. Together, you do such a great job bringing up your kids – who are two very special individuals I am proud to know, and whose care I am lucky enough to be involved with.

To Annalisa Barbieri – collaborating on the podcast as part of your series *Conversations with Annalisa Barbieri*, to record an episode on blended families, was a fantastic opportunity for me. Thank you so much for inviting me to work with you on it. In fact, it was listening to it that was the catalyst for Headline getting in touch in the first place – so little did I know it would lead to another chance to spread the word about the importance of taking care of the step/blended families so many of us are a part of!

To all the people who contributed their experiences of being part of a step or blended family. We make meaning through sharing our stories and helping each other make sense of what we go through. I am honoured you have allowed *Step Up* to give voice to your own difficult experiences and top tips to help the many others who are in similar situations.

To the Centre for Counselling and Psychotherapy Education (CCPE), London. Completing the majority of my therapeutic trainings here has been one of the highlights of my life – which I'm aware is a big statement to make! But it's true. It's not just the high quality of the teaching, which is even more notable and important in a world where our profession isn't regulated. This starkly contrasts with others where the focus is solely on classroom learning or is too short to really help students really get to grips with their own processes, to be of true service to their clients. It's in the focus on group work – and blended families are nothing if not a masterclass in group dynamics. It's the focus on experiential learning. It's in the fabric of the building which provides such a safe haven for so many. It's in the community that has been developed over 40 years, and the teaching has evolved since then. And it's in the safety of the rooms that hold so many secrets, where people pour their hearts out week after week about their own experiences in step-families and so much more, to experienced guides who have trained for years to help you to make sense of your life without polluting your process with theirs. I could go on. But suffice to say my experience and learning at CCPE has ultimately underpinned every page in this book.

To those who have taken the time to generously endorse *Step Up* and to those who may go on to do so in the future. Your thumbs up for the messages in this book means that many more people may be inspired to read *Step Up* as a result of your recommendation than otherwise may have.

Katherine Walker
MA. Dip. Psych, Dip. Coup., Dip. Spvn, Adv. Dip. Coach., Dip. Med.
Founder | Curious & Brave Ltd.
Psychotherapy, Coaching & Mediation